Usin
the e

CW01401726

Books Available

By both authors:
BP327 DOS one step at a time
BP337 A Concise User's Guide to Lotus 1-2-3 for Windows
BP341 MS-DOS explained
BP346 Programming in Visual Basic for Windows
BP352 Excel 5 explained
BP362 Access one step at a time
BP387 Windows one step at a time
BP388 Why not personalise your PC
BP400 Windows 95 explained
BP406 MS Word 95 explained
BP407 Excel 95 explained
BP408 Access 95 one step at a time
BP409 MS Office 95 one step at a time
BP415 Using Netscape on the Internet*
BP420 E-mail on the Internet*
BP426 MS-Office 97 explained
BP428 MS-Word 97 explained
BP429 MS-Excel 97 explained
BP430 MS-Access 97 one step at a time
BP433 Your own Web site on the Internet
BP448 Lotus SmartSuite 97 explained
BP456 Windows 98 explained*
BP460 Using Microsoft Explorer 4 on the Internet*
BP464 E-mail and news with Outlook Express*
BP465 Lotus SmartSuite Millennium explained
BP471 Microsoft Office 2000 explained
BP472 Microsoft Word 2000 explained
BP473 Microsoft Excel 2000 explained
BP474 Microsoft Access 2000 explained
BP478 Microsoft Works 2000 explained
BP486 Using Linux the easy way*
BP488 Internet Explorer 5 explained*
BP491 Windows 2000 explained*

By Noel Kantaris:
BP258 Learning to Program in C
BP259 A Concise Introduction to UNIX*
BP284 Programming in QuickBASIC
BP325 A Concise User's Guide to Windows 3.1

Using Linux
the easy way

by

N. Kantaris
and
P.R.M. Oliver

**Bernard Babani (publishing) Ltd
The Grampians
Shepherds Bush Road
London W6 7NF
England**

Please Note

Although every care has been taken with the production of this book to ensure that any projects, designs, modifications and/or programs, etc., contained herewith, operate in a correct and safe manner and also that any components specified are normally available in Great Britain, the Publishers and Author(s) do not accept responsibility in any way for the failure (including fault in design) of any project, design, modification or program to work correctly or to cause damage to any equipment that it may be connected to or used in conjunction with, or in respect of any other damage or injury that may be so caused, nor do the Publishers accept responsibility in any way for the failure to obtain specified components.

Notice is also given that if equipment that is still under warranty is modified in any way or used or connected with home-built equipment then that warranty may be void.

British Library Cataloguing in Publication Data:

A catalogue record for this book is available from the British Library

ISBN 0 85934 486 X

Cover Design by Gregor Arthur
Printed and Bound in Great Britain by Bath Press

About this Book

Using Linux the easy way was written to help both the beginner and those upgrading from older versions of Linux. The material in the book is presented on the 'what you need to know first, appears first' basis, although you don't have to start at the beginning and go right through to the end. The more experienced user can start from any section, as they have been designed to be self-contained.

Linux is a 32-bit operating system with the latest versions having a Graphical User Interface (GUI) front end, and includes built-in accessories like a text editor, paint program and many other multimedia, networking and electronic communication features, some of which are examined in this book. Getting to grips with Linux and its GUI, as described, will also reduce the learning curve when it comes to using other Linux application packages. For example, once you have learned how to install a new printer, you should never again have any difficulty printing from any Linux utility or application program. Also, learning to manipulate text and graphics in KEdit and Paint will lay very strong foundations on which to build expertise when you need to master a fully blown word processor with elements of desktop publishing.

The latest versions of Linux come with an 'X Window System' and the GNU utilities which includes everything that one needs to write and run programs written in C. These facilities, together with the KDE (the K Desktop Environment) and the ability of the latest versions of Linux to automatically sense and install peripherals, such as printers, scanners, modems, etc., make Linux a very worth while operating system for single desktop (or networked) users, as well as developers.

If, however, you enjoy using the command line to enter instructions, you still can. We outline the process and cover the main Linux commands, but we have not attempted to cover this part of the subject fully. If you don't work that way already (because you prefer a Windows type environment), you certainly should not start now.

An attempt has been made not to use too much 'jargon' in this book, but with this subject, some is inevitable, so a fairly detailed glossary of terms is included in the last chapter, which should be used with the text whenever necessary.

The book was written with the busy person in mind. You don't need to read many hundreds of large format pages to find out most of what there is to know about the subject, when fewer pages can get you going quite adequately! It is hoped that with the help of this book, you will be able to get the most out of your computer, when using Linux, in terms of efficiency and productivity, and that you will be able to do it in the shortest, most effective and enjoyable way.

If you would like to purchase a Companion Disc for any of the books, by the same author(s), in the Books Available list, **apart from this one and the ones marked with an asterisk**, containing the file/program listings which appear in them, then fill in the form at the back of the book and send it to Phil Oliver at the stipulated address.

About the Authors

Noel Kantaris graduated in Electrical Engineering at Bristol University and after spending three years in the Electronics Industry in London, took up a Tutorship in Physics at the University of Queensland. Research interests in Ionospheric Physics, led to the degrees of M.E. in Electronics and Ph.D. in Physics. On return to the UK, he took up a Post-Doctoral Research Fellowship in Radio Physics at the University of Leicester, and then in 1973 a lecturing position in Engineering at the Camborne School of Mines, Cornwall, (part of Exeter University), where between 1978 and 1997 he was also the CSM Computing Manager. At present he is IT Director of FFC Ltd.

Phil Oliver graduated in Mining Engineering at Camborne School of Mines in 1967 and since then has specialised in most aspects of surface mining technology, with a particular emphasis on computer related techniques. He has worked in Guyana, Canada, several Middle Eastern and Asian countries, South Africa and the United Kingdom, on such diverse projects as: the planning and management of bauxite, iron, gold and coal mines; rock excavation contracting in the UK; international mining equipment sales and international mine consulting. In 1988 he took up a lecturing position at Camborne School of Mines (part of Exeter University) in Surface Mining and Management. He retired from full-time lecturing in 1998, to spend more time writing, consulting and developing Web sites for clients.

Acknowledgements

We would like to thank the technical support staff of Linux SuSE, for their helpful tips and suggestions which assisted us in the writing of this book.

Trademarks

HP and LaserJet are registered trademarks of Hewlett Packard Corporation.

IBM is a registered trademark of International Business Machines, Inc.

Intel is a registered trademark of Intel Corporation.

Microsoft, **MS-DOS**, **Windows**, and **Windows NT**, are either registered trademarks or trademarks of Microsoft Corporation.

PostScript is a registered trademark of Adobe Systems Incorporated.

All other brand and product names used in the book are recognised as trademarks, or registered trademarks, of their respective companies.

Contents

1

Introduction

Linux came into being when in 1991 the Finish student Linus Torvalds started programming his own PC version of UNIX. He then published both the executable and the source codes of his efforts on the Internet and invited other programmers to improve on it. The only stipulation he made was that such improvements should also be published on the Internet. The addition of the XFree86 code, which is an 'X Window System' for PC-based UNIX systems, made Linux desirable not only to home PC users, but also to the server market.

However, what made Linux a usable development environment was the GNU utilities that Richard Stallman (the author of the famous Emacs editor), started to write for the UNIX system back in 1983. The GNU utilities comprised everything that one needed to write and run programs written in C, including an editor, a shell, a C compiler, linker, assembler, debugger, etc. Again, the intention was to publish freely all these utilities and get other programmers to improve their code.

Thus Linux has been driven from the start by non-commercial interests, hence its popularity. It costs nothing to obtain this operating system. You can download it from the Internet, get it on a CD from various PC magazines, or obtain it from various distribution houses, such as SuSE, Red Hat, or Caldera, to mention but a few. Getting Linux from such distribution houses will cost you between £20 and £50, but then you are sure you are getting the latest boxed version of the program, with additional material on several CDs, plus sizeable documentation (more about this later).

We have mentioned that Linux is a version of UNIX, so we will cover briefly the history of UNIX for those who would like to know the details, before we continue with Linux.

The UNIX operating system was first developed in the early 1970s at AT&T's Bell Laboratories in the United States. Since then more than twenty variants of the original have appeared as the concept has gained popularity. Efforts had been made to agree on a standard that will run on anything from a mainframe to a PC, regardless of the manufacturer of the hardware. The American National Standards Institute (ANSI) drew up specifications for a look-alike UNIX operating system to be known by the name of Posix.

Some time later, IBM, DEC, HP and others, formed the Open Systems Foundation (OSF), in an attempt to develop the definitive standard for UNIX, based on IBM's own version of the system, called AIX. Sun Microsystems, on the other hand, forged ahead with their own version of UNIX, first with SunOS and later with Solaris.

UNIX's popularity rested on the fact that it would run on endless different makes of computers. Writing a program in a portable language, such as C (the language UNIX itself is written in), and then being able to run these programs on any computer under UNIX without any change whatsoever is very attractive indeed. Hence, the popularity of UNIX, and now Linux which is an independent Posix implementation.

Linux, like UNIX, can run in both multitasking and multi-user modes. Multitasking means running several programs at the same time on the same computer, while multi-user means that several people who are connected to the same network can run the same, or different, programs that might be residing on the network's server. Above all, users turn to Linux (or UNIX) for its stability, greater security, and superior performance. In addition, Linux is free, whether you are running it on your home PC or on all the PCs in your company! Currently it is installed in around 10 million PCs.

Finally, Linux can coexist with other operating systems, such as DOS, Windows 9x and higher, or Windows NT/2000. The latest Linux distributions come with powerful set-up tools which automatically recognise your hardware and display a menu-driven graphical installer to help even the first-time user to complete their set-up and have the program's desktop environment up and running in a very short time.

As mentioned earlier, Linux is available from the Internet, from CD's given away with PC magazines, or from various distribution houses. With the first two outlets, don't expect documentation or technical support. On the other hand, many of the major distribution companies not only provide you with an intelligent graphical installer, thus making the set-up of Linux as friendly as possible, but also include a host of utilities, editors, file managers, multimedia tools, support for fax and e-mail and a bundle of other packages.

For example, the SuSE and Red Hat distributions (USA edition only) come with the latest full version of StarOffice, while the UK editions of SuSE and Caldera, for example, come with a full version of Corel WordPerfect. Such distributions come with their own installation programs, utilities, commercial software, and the popular Linux graphical user interface (GUI), called KDE (the K Desktop Environment), which is standard to all boxed distributions. All this software comes on several CDs, together with extensive documentation (500+ pages), an installation procedure manual, and technical support for a specified period.

Although we have used the latest SuSE distribution (currently version 6.4) to install Linux, apart from the specific installation process described, the book can be used with other Linux distributions as they all tend to use the same desktop environment, the most popular being the KDE. It is the ability to handle and control this desktop environment that is the main aim of this book, although we cover several other topics, including the ability to connect to and surf the Internet, and use e-mail.

Cheaper distributions of Linux, on the other hand, might only be provided on one CD with no graphical user interface, or additional software, and certainly no documentation. In such cases you are limited to typing commands into the command line editor which is similar to typing commands at the MS-DOS prompt. Such commands will be discussed throughout the book, when appropriate, even if you intend to work solely with KDE, as certain processes can not be performed without typing in an appropriate command into the command line editor.

Defining Linux

The 'real Linux' is the *kernel* (the core) of every UNIX Operating System (OS), but the kernel alone does not make the OS usable; one needs a selection of software programs known as 'tools'. For Linux, these tools are available free in their GNU versions which offer enhanced features over the original UNIX tools, such as the Emacs editor and the C/C++ compiler. The last tool compiles an application written in the high level computer language C or C++ into machine code that can be understood and run by Linux in your computer.

Together with the above, Linux can include a server Graphical User Interface (GUI), called XFree86, which is an X Windows version for PC-based UNIX systems. This program allows PCs connected to a network to display a similar GUI on their screens, even if these computers are of different type. The addition of two graphical PC desktops, KDE and GNOME, various free file management tools, applications software and games, make up the complete system known as Linux. Different distributions can include the core of Linux, plus a selection of the other free software, and a convenient set-up program.

Hardware Requirements

As Linux is a 32-bit operating system, you might be forgiven if you think that you require the latest and most powerful PC before you can use it. This, however, is not true.

A bare minimal installation of Linux only requires a 486 PC, with preferably 16 MB of RAM, but at least 150 MB of available contiguous free disc space. However, with such a minimal installation you will be limited to entering commands into the command line editor. You can compile and run programs written in C (or perhaps C++), but you will find the performance of other free applications software that come with the different distributions rather sluggish; you will also need extra hard disc space to accommodate such extra application software.

To run Linux effectively with a graphical user interface, software for Internet access, printing, CD player, games, etc., you will need a Pentium-based PC (to get the performance) with at least 32 MB of RAM and a minimum of 500 MB of free disc space. To take advantage of some of the more sophisticated free application software that comes with the large distributions, you will also need an additional 500 MB of disc space. However, if you want to install everything that comes on a 6 CD distribution, such as SuSE, and take advantage of all the available free software, then you will need at least 6 GB of free disc space! Also, to run some of the more sophisticated application software you will need 64 MB of RAM; the more you have the quicker will be the response of your system. Finally, having a CD-ROM drive and a mouse will make life a lot easier, the first with the installation of the extensive list of software and the second with the running of Linux.

Normally, large distributions allow you to install a 'minimal' or 'standard' system that you can add to later from lists of 'additional software' and 'commercial software'. In the 'additional software' list you will find games, and programs for multimedia, development, networking, Internet access and a choice between two GUIs; KDE or GNOME. In this way you can maximise your requirements and balance them against the available disc space of your system.

System Preparation

Before you start installing Linux you need to prepare your system. There are several things you have to do here.

- If your system is to run Linux only, or Linux is to be installed on a separate, but bootable, hard disc, then you don't need any preparation; you can skip the rest of this section.

- If your system has only one hard disc on which you have another operating system installed and you intend to retain it, then you need to consider the following:

1. If your hard disc is partitioned into, say, a C: and a D: drive, then move all the programs and data you want to retain from drive D: into drive C:, and use the space on drive D: to install Linux as long as there is enough space. Application programs under Windows 9x might have to be uninstalled from drive D:, and reinstalled in drive C:.

2. If your hard disc is not partitioned and you have enough free space at the end of it to load Linux, then you have two choices:

    i.   Use the commercial software package PartitionMagic to create a partition for Linux on your hard disc. Such a program partitions your hard drive without any loss of data.

    ii. Use the *fips* utility supplied with some distributions of Linux to create a suitable partition for Linux at the end of the drive, but defragment your drive before you start. However, most defragmenting software cannot move hidden or system files which might exist within the area where Linux is to be loaded, in which case you might overwrite them, so **make a backup** before you start.

3. If you have more than two partitions on your hard drive, none of which is big enough to load Linux, then make a **complete backup** of your hard drive, then either

    i.   use PartitionMagic to rearrange and/or delete such partitions to create a sufficiently large partition for Linux, or

    ii. use the *fdisk* utility to re-partition the drive into more suitable sizes, then restore your application programs and data as necessary.

Finally, before you proceed with the installation of Linux, make sure you have made a 'boot disc' for the operating system you want to retain, be it DOS, Windows 9x, Windows NT/2000, or whatever.

Yet Another Decision

Linux distributions come with a choice of set-up programs for different computers; which one you use depends on your system. For example, for older computers that cannot boot from the CD-ROM drive, or the display does not conform with the VESA 2.0 standard, you use a text-based installer which for a PC-based computer you start in DOS mode. With the SuSE distribution this installer is called YaST (Yet another Setup Tool!).

For Pentium-based PCs, you can use a graphical installer; with the SuSE distribution this is called YaST2, while in the case of the Red Hat distribution it is called GTK+. These programs not only support a genuine graphical user interface, but can also detect your hardware automatically.

The final decision is how to make Linux bootable. You need to specify at which point in the system the boot manager LILO (LInux LOader) is to be installed. The three available solutions are:

1. On the C: drive in the 'Master Boot Record' (MBR), if Linux is to be installed as the only operating system, or if you also intend to boot a number of other operating systems, such as Microsoft Windows for a PC-based computer.

2. Create a floppy boot disc and use it to boot Linux. This method is preferable if you use a number of other operating systems on the same computer and you want to leave your current boot mechanism intact. With the SuSE distribution you can use the YaST program to install LILO in the MBR at a later date.

3. On the /boot directory in the drive you selected to install Linux. However, this method is not as easy as the other two, because you are required to re-configure your existing boot manager on your own. Full details on how to do this should be found in the reference manuals of your distribution.

In our case, as we will be installing the SuSE Linux distribution on a Pentium desktop PC with Windows 98 as the other operating system, we will use the CD-ROM boot option and the YaST2 version of the installer. In addition we will create a floppy boot disc, so as not to change our current boot mechanism.

In this way, if we start our PC with the Linux boot disc in the floppy drive, the system will load Linux, otherwise it will load our current operating system.

Note: Whatever method you choose to install Linux on your computer, or how to boot it, make sure you make a complete backup of your hard disc before you begin. This cannot be overemphasised.

2

Installing Linux

To take advantage of the graphical installer, you need to make your computer bootable from the CD-ROM drive. To do this, switch your computer on, insert the Linux distribution disc containing the install program you want to use, then exit your present operating system, and switch off your PC.

Next, switch on your PC, and while the boot program is checking the PC's memory, press the <Del> key (or whatever key you are told by your PC - it appears at the bottom of the screen) to enter the CMOS SETUP UTILITY program, shown below.

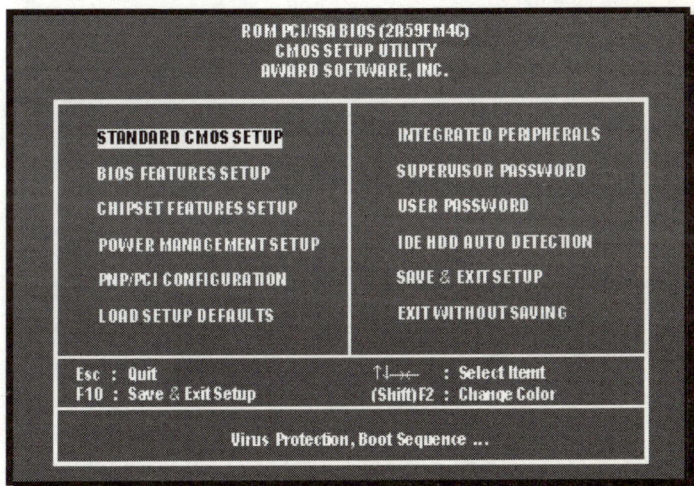

ROM PCI/ISA BIOS (2A59FM4C)
CMOS SETUP UTILITY
AWARD SOFTWARE, INC.

STANDARD CMOS SETUP	INTEGRATED PERIPHERALS
BIOS FEATURES SETUP	SUPERVISOR PASSWORD
CHIPSET FEATURES SETUP	USER PASSWORD
POWER MANAGEMENT SETUP	IDE HDD AUTO DETECTION
PNP/PCI CONFIGURATION	SAVE & EXIT SETUP
LOAD SETUP DEFAULTS	EXIT WITHOUT SAVING

Esc : Quit   ↑↓→← : Select Item
F10 : Save & Exit Setup   (Shift) F2 : Change Color

Virus Protection, Boot Sequence ...

Fig. 2.1 The CMOS Setup Utility Screen

From here, select the BIOS FEATURES SETUP option. Under 'Boot Sequence' select CDROM, C, A, by pressing the <Page Down> key until this sequence appears on the screen. Finally, press the <Esc> key to return to the previous screen (Fig. 2.1), and select the SAVE & EXIT SETUP option.

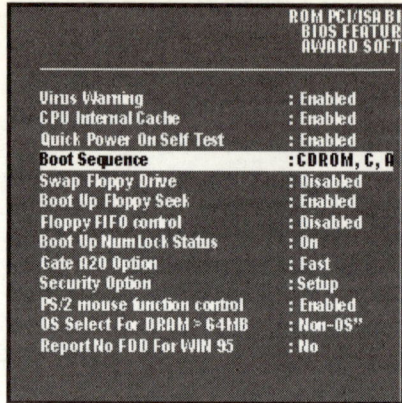

ROM PCI/ISA BI	
BIOS FEATUR	
AWARD SOFT	
Virus Warning	: Enabled
CPU Internal Cache	: Enabled
Quick Power On Self Test	: Enabled
Boot Sequence	: CDROM, C, A
Swap Floppy Drive	: Disabled
Boot Up Floppy Seek	: Enabled
Floppy FIFO control	: Disabled
Boot Up NumLock Status	: On
Gate A20 Option	: Fast
Security Option	: Setup
PS/2 mouse function control	: Enabled
OS Select For DRAM > 64MB	: Non-OS"
Report No FDD For WIN 95	: No

Fig. 2.2 Boot Sequence

Your PC should now restart automatically, and after the memory check, will boot from the CD-ROM drive, displaying the screen below.

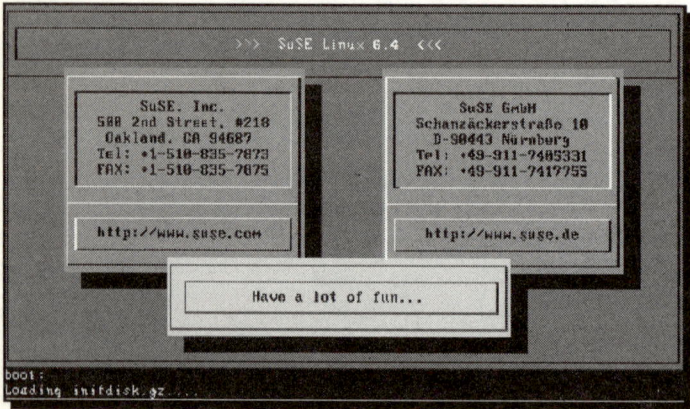

Fig. 2.3 The Start Screen of SuSE Linux

If your PC is unable to boot from the CD-ROM drive, then you must insert the 'Bootdisk' supplied by your Linux distribution into the floppy drive, restart your computer and enter the CMOS SETUP UTILITY, then change the 'Boot Sequence' to A, C, CDROM. Now your computer will boot from the supplied floppy and the same screen will appear.

Note the boot prompt 'boot:' at the bottom of the screen. After a short time the message 'Loading Linux ...' will appear below it, and a few seconds later the Linux Kernel will be booted - you will recognise this by the many messages which scroll up your screen. A few seconds later, and if you have booted from the CD-ROM drive, the following graphic interface will be displayed:

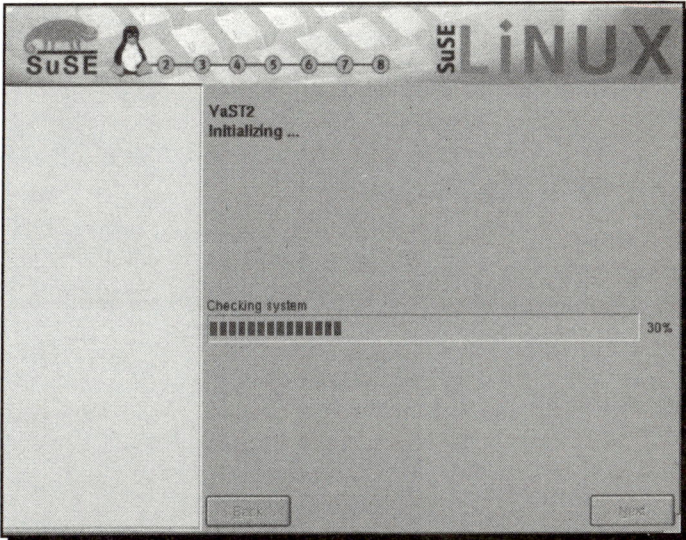

Fig. 2.4 The YaST2 Install Program

This is the YaST2 install program which will detect your hardware automatically. If, on the other hand you booted your PC from the supplied 'Bootdisk', then the displayed screen will be in text mode and you will have to supply information about your hardware; this is the YaST install program, and if you have to use it, then we suggest you follow the supplied documentation carefully, as we will not cover this aspect of it.

So, for the time being we will assume that your system has indeed booted from the CD-ROM drive and the screen shown above is displayed. From the next screen, shown overleaf, you can select the Language to be used.

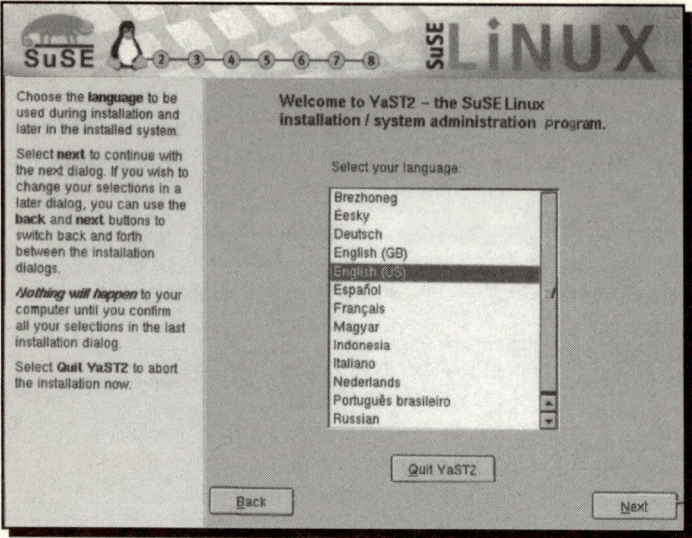

Fig. 2.5 The YaST2 Installation Methods

After selecting the Language to be used, press the **Next** button to display the Basic Configuration screen, part of which is shown below.

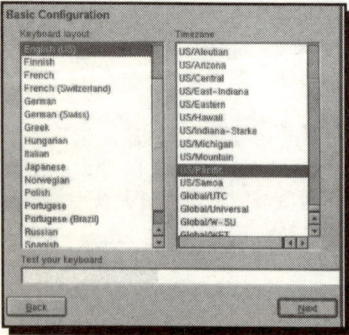

Fig. 2.6 The YaST2 Basic Configuration Screen

It is from this screen that you select the Keyboard layout and the Time Zone to be used. You can even test your keyboard by typing a few selected characters, such as "£\@~# to see if they are displayed correctly. If everything is as it should be, click the **Next** button to display the next installation screen which asks you to select between **New installation** or **Update an existing system**.

Selecting the first option allows the Install program to make all the decisions (as far as possible) for you. For example,

- if more than one hard drive is detected, you will be asked to decide on which one you wish to install Linux

- if more than one partition is detected on the selected drive, you will be asked to specify which partition to use.

Note: Make sure that you do not click the **Use entire hard disk** button on the next displayed screen, unless you really mean it, as all information on the selected drive will be lost.

Next, the Install program will check the selected hard drive and specified partition to see if there is enough space for a partition, and will format the specified hard drive space automatically. This area is split into three standard partitions; a small one (about 16 MB) for /boot, a 128 MB swap partition, and the rest for the root (/) partition in which the programs that make up your Linux installation can be stored. These programs can be selected on the following screen.

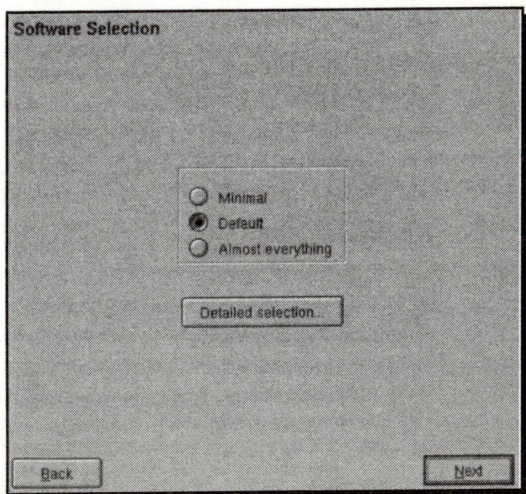

Fig. 2.7 The YaST2 Software Selection

You can use this screen to specify a 'Minimal', 'Default', or 'Almost everything' basic software installation, and clicking the **Detailed selection** button you can specify additional software such as Network/Server or Commercial software. Do remember that with a minimal installation you will only get the Linux system in text mode.

A 'Default' installation, without any selection from the additional software option, will include everything you need to start Linux, such as graphical desktop interfaces, editors, printing, software for Internet access and use, CD players, etc. The hard disc space required for such an installation is at least 500 MB, while selection of items from the additional software list will add to the hard disc space requirement.

Next, and depending on your installation choice, the LILO (LInux LOader) program might ask you where to install itself; hard drive, a floppy, or the /boot partition (refer to the end of Chapter 1 where these three methods were discussed).

Then, the program displays a screen in which it asks you to enter some personal details, such as name and surname, user login (it can be a short combination of part of your name and surname - case sensitive), and a password (also case sensitive).

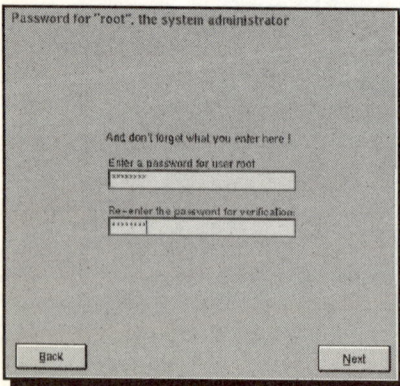

Fig. 2.8 The YaST2 Screen for Entering the 'root' password

Next, the screen to the left is displayed in which you are asked to enter the password for 'root'. This is for the system administrator who controls many tasks that ordinary users can not control. Make sure that you remember the 'root' password, because you can not see it or change it later.

As we have mentioned in Chapter 1, Linux is a multi-user system. It has to have only *one* administrator or super-user, which in this distribution is called 'root'. Only 'root' can carry out changes to the installation, add other users, and power down the system. 'Root' presides above all other users.

Finally the Install program displays a 'Confirmation' screen of the proposed changes to your system. If you like what is suggested, press the **Next** button, otherwise press the **Abort installation** button. This is the only time you are given a chance to abort installation, but you are allowed to save your settings to a floppy disc for later use.

If you continue with the installation, YaST2 will create the necessary partitions, format them and start transferring software packages from CD1. Depending on your choice and disc capacity, the Install program will ask you to insert additional CDs in your CD-ROM drive. After all the selected programs have been transferred from CD1, LILO will be installed (in our case on a floppy disc).

There are only two things left to be done.

- First, the Install program tries to detect information about your graphics card and monitor in order to configure the *X-server*, so that Linux can display a graphical user interface, even at first *Login*. If your monitor is not detected automatically, YaST2 displays a **Configure Monitor** screen with a list of monitors for you to choose from. If your monitor is not listed, then select VESA from the list, as most monitors comply to that standard.

- Second, the **System Component Configuration** screen is displayed giving you the ability to configure your Printer, Sound, Internet, and Network, as shown overleaf in Fig. 2.9. If your printer was not switched on when you first started the Linux installation, YaST2 will not detect it, so you will have to configure it by pressing the **Configure Printer** button on the displayed screen (see Fig. 2.9). This causes YaST2 to auto detect your printer.

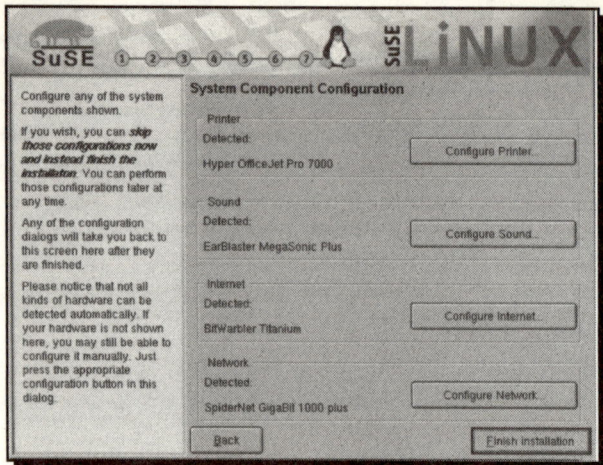

Fig. 2.9 The YaST2 System Components Configuration

Next, the 'Welcome to Linux' screen is displayed (Fig. 2.10). Note there are two entries on this *Login* screen; 'you', and 'root'. If you *login* in order to browse the Internet, send an e-mail or write a letter, then there is no reason to *login* as 'root', 'administrator', or 'super-user' (depending on the Linux distribution). You only *login* as 'root', if you intend to carry out some system management, including shutting down Linux.

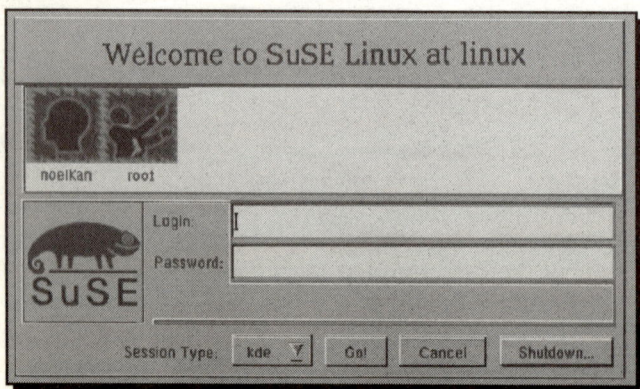

Fig. 2.10 The YaST2 KDE Display Manager

The Desktop User Interface

Linux has several graphical interfaces, but two have emerged as predominant; KDE and Gnome. The K Desktop Environment was started in Germany in 1966 and it has its own window manager, called KWM - all KDE application names and utilities start with K. KDE is loaded by default when using the SuSE distribution. Gnome (which stands for GNU Network Object Model Environment) on the other hand, doesn't have its own window manager, but is built around the GTK+ graphics libraries.

At present, KDE leads Gnome in terms of completeness, stability and range of applications, and integrates X and Gnome applications better than Gnome integrates X and KDE applications. Thus, customising Linux's environment with KDE is a lot easier than with Gnome. For these reasons, we have decided to discuss in detail only the KDE interface.

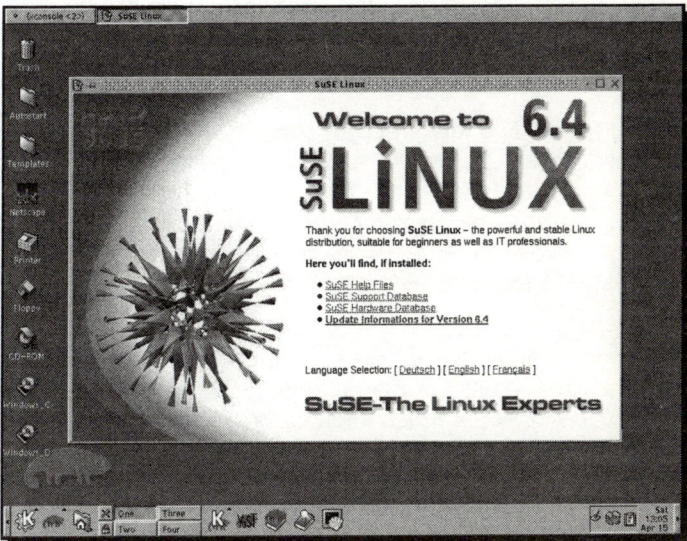

Fig. 2.11 The KDE User Interface

The Taskbar and KPanel

The empty docking bar, called Taskbar, sits at the top of the screen, while the pre-configured KPanel is at the bottom.

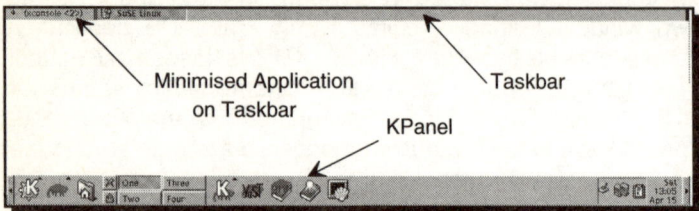

Fig. 2.12 The KDE Taskbar and KPanel

The Taskbar is where applications and windows dock when they are minimised (more about this later), but technically is part of the KPanel which is pre-configured by KDE. Starting from the left, the KPanel displays two icons with black triangles which indicates that if you left-click on one of these, it opens up a cascade menu. Those icons that do not have small black triangles on them, when left-clicked start the application associated with them.

Note: In Linux, in general, you only need to left-click an application once to start it, whether such applications are placed on the KPanel or the desktop. If you double-click by mistake, it starts two versions of the same application, which you might not always be aware of. This can be a drain on your system's resources, so be careful not to double-click!

In the next chapter, we will describe in detail the KPanel, and how to customise it. For the present, however, we will show you how to exit Linux which must be done by powering down your system. **You must never exit Linux by switching off your computer.** There are two ways to exit Linux. The first method involves typing commands in the Terminal Emulator. To do so, left-click the icon on the KPanel, shown to the left, which will display the Terminal Emulator (Fig. 2.13).

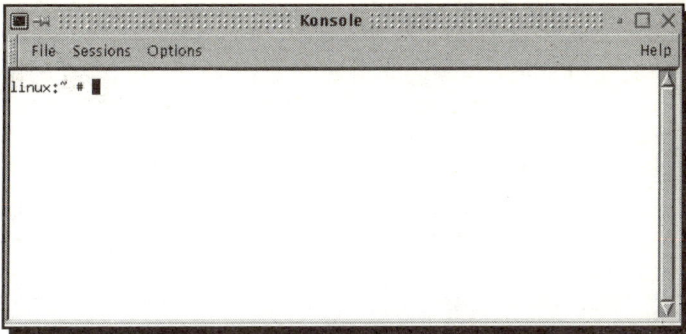

Fig. 2.13 The KDE Terminal Emulator

All you need to know, at present, is that you use the above Terminal Emulator to type in commands to the system. To exit Linux, simply type

```
shutdown -h now
```

with spaces as shown, then press the <Enter> key (the -h within the command means 'halt after shutdown'). If you want to see all the options associated with the 'shutdown' command, type

```
shutdown help
```

in the terminal emulator, which displays the following help screen:

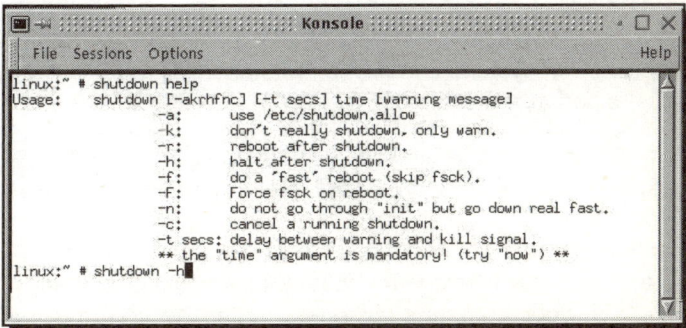

Fig. 2.14 Getting Help with Linux Commands

Next, type in the 'shutdown' command as discussed on the previous page to exit Linux. Do remember, however, that this will work only if you logged in as 'root'. If not, then left-click the Logout button on the KPanel, shown here, which will return you to the *Login* screen (Fig. 2.10), where you can login as 'root'.

This brings us to the second, and easier, method of exiting Linux. Simply click the **Shutdown** button on the *login* screen. What should happen, had you not logged in as 'root', is that the system should ask you for the 'root' password. However, the default settings cause KDE to shut down the system, whether you have logged in as 'root' or as an ordinary user! You can rectify this by invoking YaST (see Chapter 4, p.41), then selecting **System administration, Login configuration** and changing the behaviour of KDE to 'root'.

'Why', I can hear you say, 'go through the rigmarole of invoking the Terminal Emulator and typing some incomprehensible commands in order to shutdown the system, if there is an alternative and easier way of doing the same thing'? Well, there is always more than one way of doing something in Linux - the old way which involves typing in commands in the Terminal Emulator, and the new way which involves clicking a button or two on the graphical interface. We introduced both methods so that you become familiar with them, particularly the first method, as certain tasks (to be discussed later) can only be carried out by typing commands in the Terminal Emulator.

You will know that the 'shutdown' process has begun, because the system scrolls commands past your screen, until the command

```
The system will be halted immediately.
Master Resource Control: run level 0 has been reached
```

At this point, you can remove the Linux Boot Disc from the A: drive (if this was where you chose to install LILO), and either switch off your computer, or press simultaneously the key combination <Ctrl+Alt+Del> to restart your PC with the alternative Operating System.

3

The KDE User Interface

Starting Linux

To boot Linux, in our case, we simply place the Linux Boot Disc containing the Linux Loader (LILO) into the floppy drive and switch on the PC. For this to work, the 'Boot Sequence' should have been set to A,C,CDROM, as discussed at the beginning of Chapter 2. You, of course, might have selected a different way of booting Linux, in which case you must follow the procedure necessary for your chosen method.

A few seconds later the Linux Kernel will be booted, you will recognise this by the many messages which scroll up your screen, and after a short period, the 'Welcome to Linux' screen is displayed, as shown below.

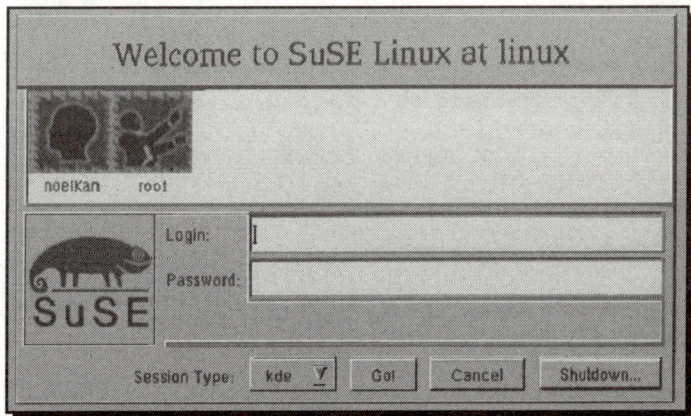

Fig. 3.1 The YaST2 KDE Display Manager

As discussed in the previous chapter, you only *login* as 'root' (the administrator, or super-user), if you intend to carry out some system management, including shutting down Linux. As we intend to explore the KDE user interface, *login* as 'yourself', in this instance, because you are less likely to do damage to your system if you do not have 'root' privileges. Linux, being a multi-user system, allows many different people to use the system without the power to affect it by deleting important system files - each user can change or delete only their own files. How this different filing system is set up for each user, will be discussed later on.

Having logged in, the KDE user interface is displayed on your screen, with desktop icons representing program applications or utilities, and the pre-configured KPanel, as shown below.

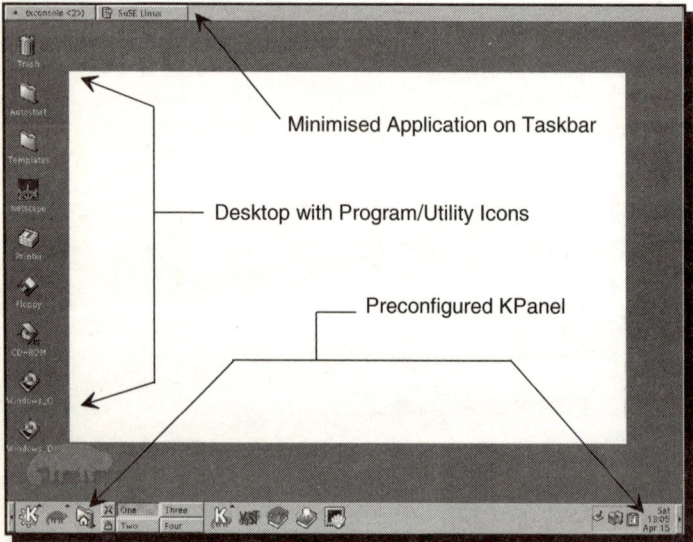

Fig. 3.2 The KDE User Interface

In the next few pages we will list the function of each icon displayed on the desktop, as well as those appearing on the pre-configured KPanel.

The Desktop Icons

The desktop icons have the following functions:

Trash

Dragging icons which represent files or folders to the Trash bin, deletes these files or folders from their usual place and puts them in the Trash bin. Such 'deleted' files or folders will remain in the Trash bin until you either restore them into their original place or empty the Trash bin. Left-clicking the Trash icon displays all the deleted items held in it.

Autostart

The Autostart folder can contain programs or links to programs that KDE runs automatically when it first starts up. Left-clicking the Autostart icon, opens the folder and displays its contents, if any.

Templates

The Templates folder holds templates that you might use to save time in producing, say, a unified layout for your letters or drawings. Left-clicking the Templates icon, opens the folder and displays its contents, if any.

Netscape

Left-clicking this icon starts the Netscape Navigator so that you can browse the Internet, provided your system is configured to do so (more about this later).

Printer

Left-clicking this icon displays the Printer dialogue box which allows you to display the state of all printers connected to the system, this allows you to easily manage the jobs queuing to be printed.

Floppy

Left-clicking this icon, mounts a Linux floppy disc in the floppy drive (only if it is a Linux floppy), and automatically accesses its contents. Once mounted, a small square appears at the bottom right corner of the icon to indicate its state (see the CD-ROM icon below). A mounted floppy disc must not be taken out of the floppy drive, unless it is first 'unmounted'. To do this, right-click the icon and select 'unmount' from the pop-up menu.

| Open with |
| Unmount |
| Copy |
| Move to Trash |
| Delete |
| Properties |

CD-ROM

Left-clicking the CD-ROM icon, mounts the CD that is inside the CD-ROM drive (only if it is a Linux CD), and automatically accesses its contents. As we already had the Linux installation CD in the CD-ROM drive before starting Linux, the CD was detected automatically and the drive mounted (indicated by the small square at the bottom right corner of the icon). Once mounted, a CD must not be taken out of the CD-ROM drive, unless you first 'unmount' it. To do this, right-click the CD-ROM icon and select 'unmount' from the pop-up menu.

Windows Drive

Left-clicking this icon, displays the contents of the hard disc drive of the alternative operating system (in this case Microsoft Windows). Linux has automatically detected the drive(s) of the other operating system and added appropriate icon(s) on the desktop.

The KPanel Icons

The KPanel icons have the following functions:

K Start

Left-clicking this icon opens up the **K Start** menu (the small upward arrow at the top right corner of the icon indicates the presence of such a pop-up menu). Holding the mouse pointer over an entry which has a small right arrow to the right of it, opens up a further cascade menu, as shown in Fig. 3.3 below. The **K Start** menu holds pre-configured Linux applications and utilities, but it is possible to add to it, as we shall see later.

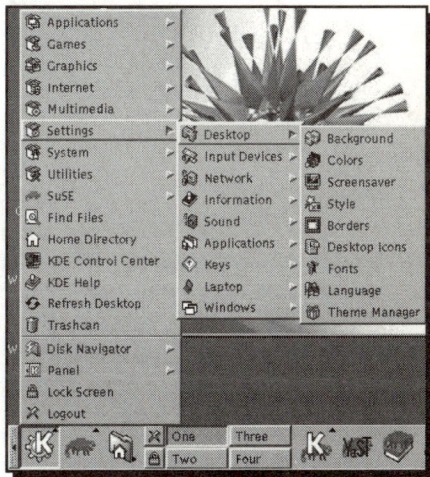

Fig. 3.3 The K Start Cascade Menu

SuSE Apps

Left-clicking this icon opens up the SuSE specific applications menu (the small upward arrow at the top right corner of the icon indicates the presence of such a menu). Holding the mouse pointer over an entry which has a small right arrow to the right of it, opens up a further menu, as shown in Fig. 3.4.

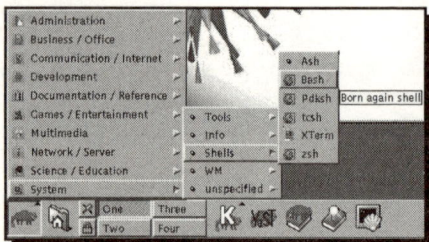

Fig. 3.4 The SuSE Applications Menus

Home

The folder containing your personal files which you can access by left-clicking this button. Each user has their own Home folder with their own personal files in it. Such a folder can be customised by each user to suit their own requirements.

Logout

Left-clicking this button allows you to *logout*. You can use this facility to perhaps *logout* in order to *login* as a different user.

Lock Screen

Left-clicking this button allows you to lock the screen. To unlock the screen, press the <Esc> key and type your password in the pop-up dialogue box.

Virtual Desktops

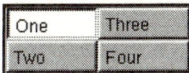

The four buttons labelled 'one' to 'four' allow you to switch between virtual desktops. KDE provides you with two methods of multitasking; you can run more than one program application in one virtual desktop or you can run different program applications in different virtual desktops. The first method is normally used if you need to have both application windows on the same desktop so that you can use the drag and drop facility, while the second method is used if it is better to run an application program full-screen, such as a word processor. Each virtual desktop is fully configurable by using the 'Display Settings' button on the KPanel, to be discussed shortly.

SuSE Work Menu

Left-clicking this icon opens up the SuSE work menu (Fig. 3.5) which, amongst other things, allows you to configure your system using the YaST2, set up the CD Player, etc.

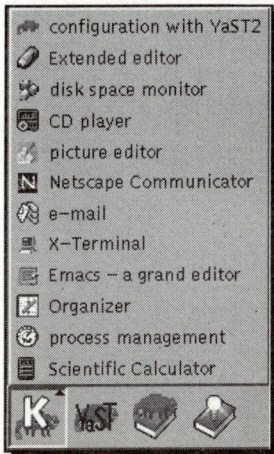

Fig. 3.5 The SuSE Work Menu

YaST Setup Tool

Left-clicking this icon starts the YaST Setup Tool. However, this only works if you have logged in as 'root', as the various options offered by this tool can change your Linux set-up.

SuSE Help

Left-clicking this icon initiates the Linux support screen, using Netscape to display the initial help pages from a local host (help files transferred onto your hard disc). However, the initial screen is in German, and to change the language you must first scroll to the bottom right-hand side of the screen and click on 'English'. Having done this, you can now see the links you can make to the World Wide Web in English. This only works if you are connected to the Internet and your system has been configured accordingly.

The Help System

Linux provides you with a complete Help System. Left-clicking this icon starts the Help program as shown in Fig. 3.6. We suggest you spend sometime going through the various help topics.

Fig. 3.6 The KDE Help System

The Shell

Linux allows you to communicate with the Linux kernel via the 'Shell' program by providing an easy way of issuing commands to the system. Left-clicking this icon, evokes the *bash* terminal emulator. The original Linux Shell was known as the 'Bourne Shell', after its originator. As this was later improved, the name *bash* was given to the current Shell, which stands for 'Bourne Again Shell'!

New Note

Left-clicking this icon opens up a 'yellow notepad' for each user to jot down short notes. These reminding notes remain in the pad until they are deleted.

Display Settings

Left-clicking this icon opens up the Display Setting dialogue box to be discussed towards the end of this chapter. Each user can use this facility to change the settings of each of their virtual desktops to their requirements. We will examine this in detail in the next section.

Clipboard History

Left-clicking on this icon opens up a screen that contains details of what has been transferred onto the clipboard.

Toggle Switch

Left-clicking this toggle switch, to be found at the extreme left (and right) of the KPanel, hides the KPanel icons so that you have a larger viewing screen, but still displays the toggle switch at the bottom of the screen and anchors the three icons (Fig. 3.7) on the Taskbar.

Fig. 3.7 The KPanel Toggled Off

An Application Window

To see a program application window, left-click (once) the Shell icon on the KPanel. This displays the *Konsole* Terminal Emulator window, as shown in Fig. 3.8 below.

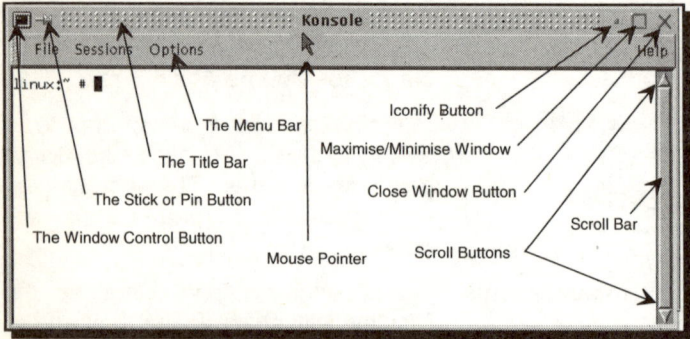

Fig. 3.8 The Terminal Emulator Window

Note the various areas and buttons on the above window. Their functions are as follows:

Area	*Function*
Window Control Button	Clicking on the program icon (at the upper-left corner of the window), displays the pull-down Window Control menu shown on the next page (Fig. 3.9) which can be used to control the program window. The pull-down menu includes commands for maximising, iconifying, moving, re-sizing, sticking or pinning the window to all desktops, sending the window to a specific desktop, and closing the window.

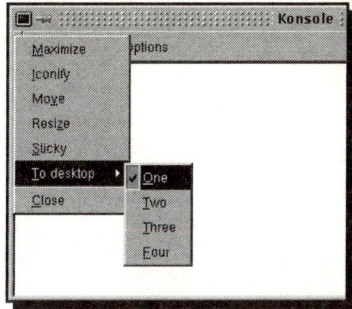

Fig. 3.9 The Window Control Menu

The Stick or Pin Button

Left-clicking on the Stick or Pin button, pins the particular window to all the virtual desktops at the selected place. Once pinned in place the icon changes shape showing a pin viewed looking down onto its head. Left-clicking the icon once more, releases the pinned window from the particular virtual desktop.

Title Bar

The bar at the top of a window which displays the name of the running application. A window can be moved around the desktop by pointing to this bar, holding down the left mouse button and dragging the window to a different place.

The Iconify Button

The button you point to and left-click to store an application as an icon on the Taskbar. Clicking on such an icon will restore the window.

Maximise Button

The button you point to and left-click to fill the screen with the active window. Left-clicking this button on a maximised window, restores the window to its former size.

Close Button

The extreme top right button that you left-click to close a window.

Menu Bar

The bar below the Title bar which allows you to choose from several menu options. Clicking on a menu item displays the pull-down menu associated with that item. The options listed in the Menu bar depend on the specific application.

Scroll Bars

The bars on the extreme right and bottom of each window that contain a scroll box. Clicking on these bars allows you to see parts of a document that might not be visible in that size window.

Scroll Buttons

The arrowheads at each end of the scroll bars which you click to scroll the window contents up and down one line, or left and right one item at a time.

Mouse pointer

The arrow which appears when the pointer is placed over menus, scrolling bars, and buttons.

The Mouse Pointers

In Linux, as with all graphical based programs and utilities, using a mouse makes many operations both easier and more fun to carry out.

Linux has several different mouse pointers, with the most common illustrated below, which it uses for its various functions. Some of these depend on the type of work you are doing at the time.

Pointer	*Function*
▶	The arrow which appears when the pointer is placed over menus, scrolling bars, and buttons.
I	The I-beam which appears in normal text areas of the screen.
✛	The four-headed pointer that appears after selecting the **Mo̲ve** option from the pull-down menu displayed when you left-click a window control button, or left-click a window with the <Alt> key depressed. This allows you to drag a window that can not be re-sized so that you can see parts of it that might be obscured.
→│ ⬐	The arrows which appear when over the border (or corner) of a window, used to drag the side (or both sides) and alter the size of the window.
✋	The Help hand which appears in the help windows, and is used to access 'hypertext' type links.

Linux applications, such as word processors, spreadsheets and databases, can have additional mouse pointers which facilitate the execution of selected commands such as highlighting text, defining areas for the appearance of charts, etc.

The Menu Bar Options

Each window's menu bar option has associated with it a pull-down sub-menu. To activate the menu of a window, use the mouse to point to an option which turns the selected option into a button. Pressing the left mouse button, reveals the pull-down sub-menu of the activated menu option. Below, we show the **Options** sub-menu of the Konsole window.

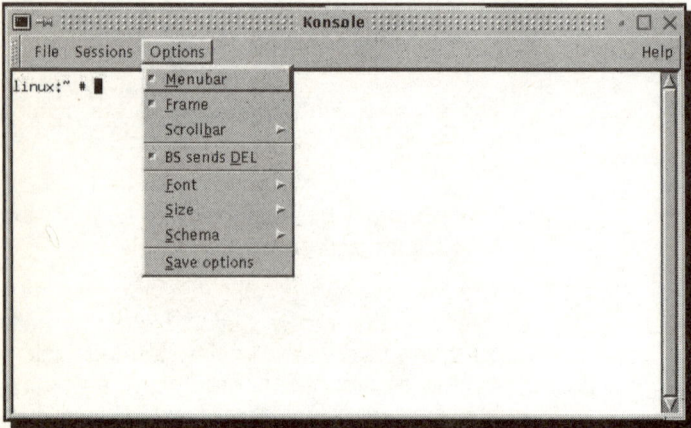

Fig. 3.10 The Sub-Menu of a Menu Option

Once an option has been activated, you can use the up and down arrow keys to move the highlighted bar up and down a sub-menu, or the right and left arrow keys to move along the options in the menu bar. Pressing the <Enter> key selects the highlighted option or executes the highlighted command. Pressing the <Esc> key once, closes the pull-down sub-menu, while pressing the <Esc> key for a second time, closes the menu system.

Items on the pull-down sub-menu which are marked with an arrow head to their right, as shown here, open up additional options when selected. Try opening one of the sub-menu options of the Konsole shown on the screen dump of Fig. 3.10. Other applications might have different items on their menu bar from the ones shown here.

Shortcut Menus

To see a shortcut menu containing the most common commands applicable to an item, point with your mouse at the item and click the right mouse button. For example, right-clicking on an empty area of the KDE desktop reveals the following options:

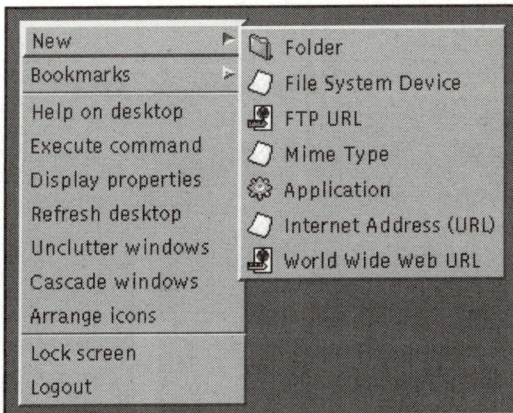

Fig. 3.11 The Desktop Shortcut Menu

In this case we can choose to create a **New** Folder, File System Device, or Internet Address, amongst several other possible sub-options. Other menu options can be selected from the list on the left column by moving the mouse downwards. Once you have highlighted a required option, left-click it to activate it.

Having activated a shortcut menu, you can close it without taking any further action by simply pressing the <Esc> key.

It might be worth your while to right-click some of the icons on your desktop in turn, to find out what the differences are between their shortcut menus. For example, you will find that with some of them you get the option to **Delete** them, but be careful before doing so.

Dialogue Boxes

To see a dialogue box, left-click the Display Settings icon on the KPanel, shown here to the left, which opens up a rather special type of screen shown below (Fig. 3.12), with an array of tabs at the top. Each tab, when left-clicked, displays a different screen (or dialogue box) for you to enter information.

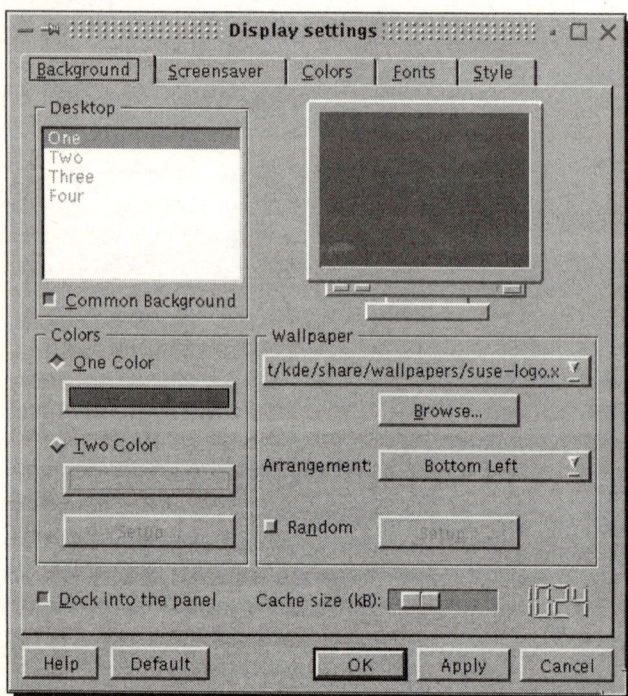

Fig. 3.12 Example of a Dialogue Box

Note: Depending on your monitor configuration the Display Settings window might not be visible in its totality on your screen. If that is the case, press and hold down the <Alt> key, then point anywhere within the window which changes the mouse pointer to the distinctive four-headed shape that can be used to drag obscured parts of the window into view.

When a display such as the one in Fig. 3.12 opens up, the <Tab> key can be used to move the dotted rectangle (known as the focus) from one field to another (Shift+<Tab> moves the focus backwards). Alternatively you can move directly to a desired field by holding the <Alt> key down and pressing the underlined letter in the field name. With the mouse, you simply point and left-click at the desired field.

Some application displays (like the one in our example on the previous page) contain List boxes which show a column of available choices (see under 'Desktop' in Fig. 3.12). If there are more choices than can be seen in the area provided, use the scroll bars to reveal them. To select a single item from a List box, either left-click the item, or use the arrow keys to highlight the item and press <Enter>.

Such displays may contain Option buttons (sometimes also called radio buttons - they used to be round) with a list of mutually exclusive items (in our example such option buttons appear under 'Colors'). The default choice is marked with the button appearing as pressed, while unavailable options are dimmed. Another type of dialogue box option is the Check box which offers a list of features you can switch on or off. Selected options show the button as pressed, like the one appearing towards the bottom of the display of our chosen example.

Having selected an option or typed in information in a text box, you must press a command button, such as the **OK**, **Cancel** or **Apply** button (unavailable options or command buttons are dimmed), or choose from additional options.

To close such a display screen, either press the **Cancel** button (some applications have a **Close** button instead), the <Esc> key, or the **X** (close) button at the top right corner of the screen.

4

Controlling the KDE Interface

Changing the Display Settings

You might like to change the KDE display settings by, perhaps, changing the colour of a virtual desktop, or by adding a screen saver. To do this, left-click the Display Settings icon on the KPanel to open up the screen below (Fig. 4.1).

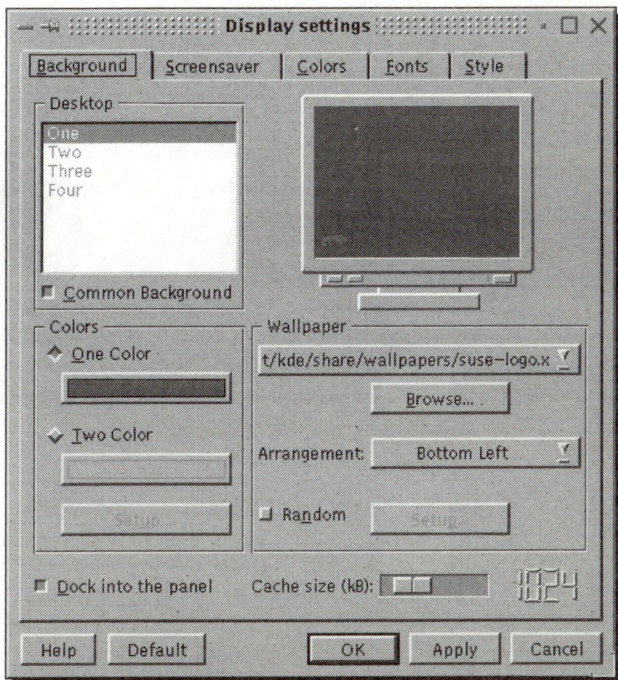

Fig. 4.1 The Display Settings Screen

With the Background tab actioned, you can select the colour for each virtual desktop, or you can choose a common background. You can also select to display a wallpaper as a background to your display. Try the various options.

Left-clicking the Screensaver tab, displays the following screen, Fig. 4.2.

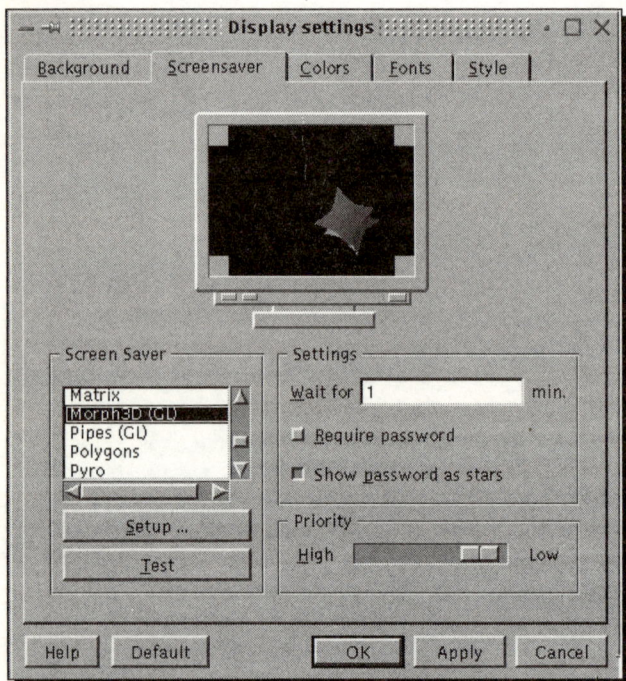

Fig. 4.2 Selecting a Screen Saver

Selecting a screen saver is a good idea, as this stops your screen showing the same display when you are not working, perhaps for hours, which can damage your monitor. The screen saver starts if your computer is idle for a specified number of minutes, and you can clear it from the screen by either moving your mouse or pressing any key on the keyboard.

Editing and Adding Users

The User Administration Tool can be used to easily edit, add, or remove users, provided you have logged in as 'root'. If not, click the logout icon on the KPanel, shown here, and *login* as 'root'.

Next, left-click the YaST icon, shown to the left, to display the YaST Setup Tool. Then select the 'System administration' option, followed by the 'User administration' option, from the cascade menu shown below in Fig. 4.3.

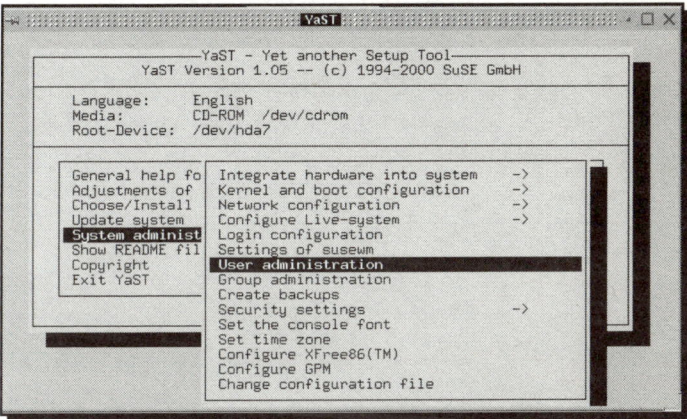

```
┌─────────────────────────YaST──────────────────────────────── □ ×
│        ┌──────────YaST - Yet another Setup Tool───────────┐
│        │   YaST Version 1.05 -- (c) 1994-2000 SuSE GmbH    │
│        │                                                   │
│        │ Language:    English                              │
│        │ Media:       CD-ROM  /dev/cdrom                   │
│        │ Root-Device: /dev/hda7                            │
│        │                                                   │
│        │ General help fo│ Integrate hardware into system  -> │
│        │ Adjustments of │ Kernel and boot configuration   -> │
│        │ Choose/Install │ Network configuration           -> │
│        │ Update system  │ Configure Live-system           -> │
│        │ System administ│ Login configuration                │
│        │ Show README fil│ Settings of susewm                 │
│        │ Copyright      │ User administration                │
│        │ Exit YaST      │ Group administration               │
│        │                │ Create backups                     │
│        │                │ Security settings               -> │
│        │                │ Set the console font               │
│        │                │ Set time zone                      │
│        │                │ Configure XFree86(TM)              │
│        │                │ Configure GPM                      │
│        │                │ Change configuration file          │
└─────────────────────────────────────────────────────────────
```

Fig. 4.3 Starting the User Administration Tool

This opens up the User Administration dialogue screen, shown in Fig 4.4, which allows you to find information relating to a current user, add a user, or delete a user.

To edit information relating to a current user, either type his/her name in the highlighted text box labelled 'User name', or press the **F3** function key then select the user from the displayed list. Unfortunately the list obtained using **F3**, not only includes the names of real users, but also the names of certain folders! So, it is better to search for users by typing in their user name.

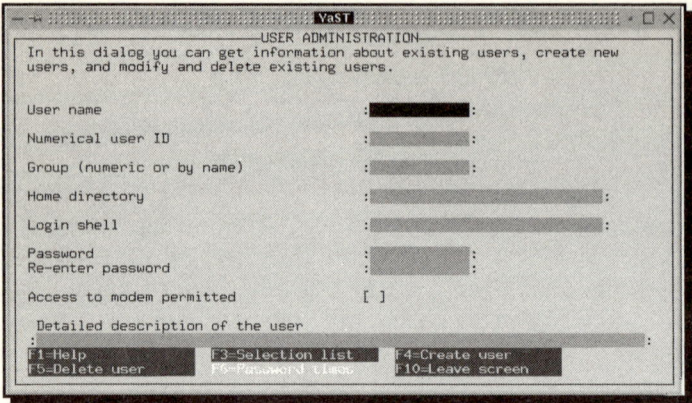

Fig. 4.4 The User Administration Screen

In Fig. 4.5 below, we show the information held for user 'noelkan' which we created during installation. All we had to do to get this information was to type in the user name.

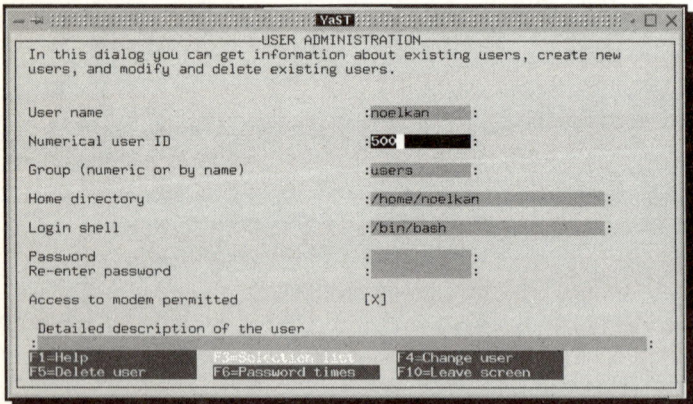

Fig. 4.5 The User Properties Dialogue Box

You could add the full name of this user in the 'Detailed description of the user' text box - perhaps you could also include additional personal information.

To change user, or add a new user, press the **F4** function key which allows you to replace the name of the previous user on the form with a new entry. In Fig. 4.6 we have typed in the name of a new user, called 'fred', his chosen password, and his full name. The rest of the information on the form was filled in automatically by the system.

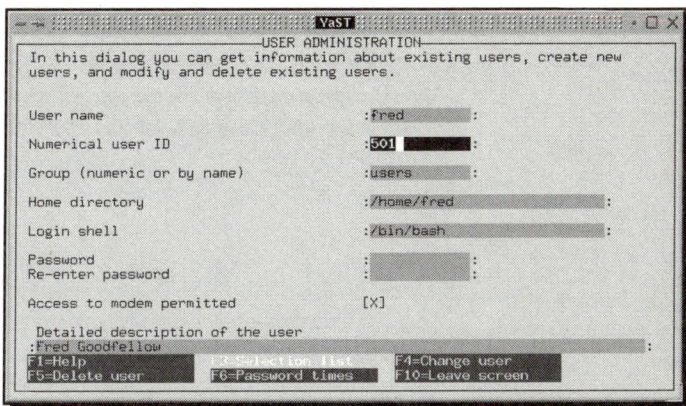

Fig. 4.6 Adding a User in the Properties Dialogue Box

Pressing the **F4** function key once more, saves your entry to the User Administration list. Next time you access the KDE Display Manager, you will find that the user 'fred', has been added as shown below in Fig. 4.7.

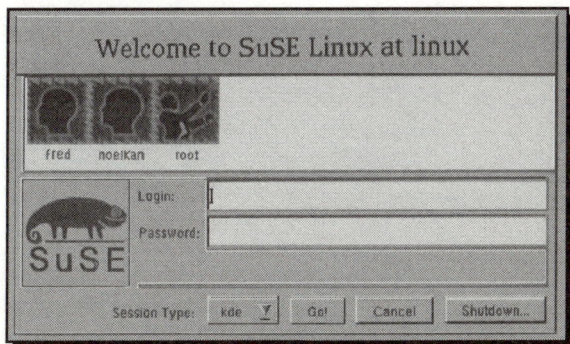

Fig. 4.7 The Changed YaST2 KDE Display Manager

Configuring or Changing a Printer

If you did not have your printer switched on during the Linux installation, or you have changed your printer since then, you will need to reconfigure. To do this, you must be logged in as 'root', then left-click the SuSE Work Menu icon on the KPanel, shown to the left, to display the pop-up menu below (Fig. 4.8).

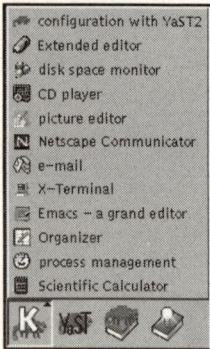

Click on the **configuration with YaST2** option at the very top of the menu, which displays the screen shown in Fig.4.9.

configuration with YaST2
Extended editor
disk space monitor
CD player
picture editor
Netscape Communicator
e-mail
X-Terminal
Emacs – a grand editor
Organizer
process management
Scientific Calculator

Fig. 4.8 The SuSE Work Menu

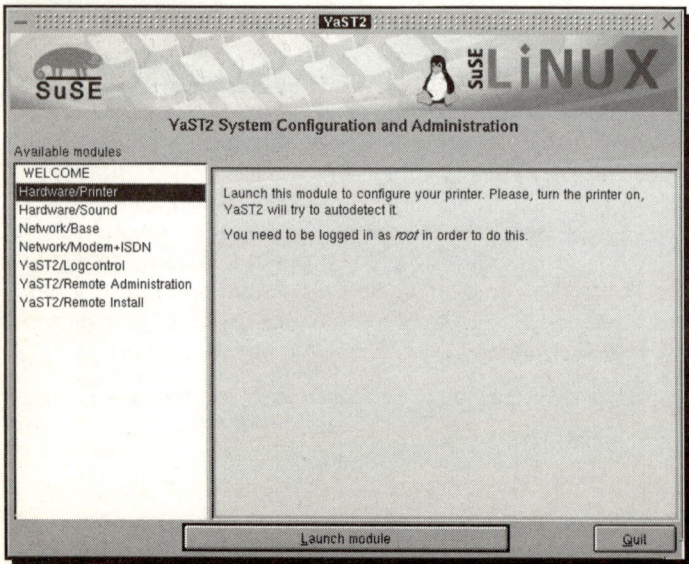

YaST2

SuSE   SuSE LINUX

YaST2 System Configuration and Administration

Available modules

WELCOME
Hardware/Printer
Hardware/Sound
Network/Base
Network/Modem+ISDN
YaST2/Logcontrol
YaST2/Remote Administration
YaST2/Remote Install

Launch this module to configure your printer. Please, turn the printer on, YaST2 will try to autodetect it.

You need to be logged in as *root* in order to do this.

Launch module   Quit

Fig. 4.9 The YaST2 System Configuration Screen

Pressing the **Launch module** bar at the bottom of the System Configuration screen, autodetects your printer, or additional printers that might be connected to your system, as shown in Fig. 4.10.

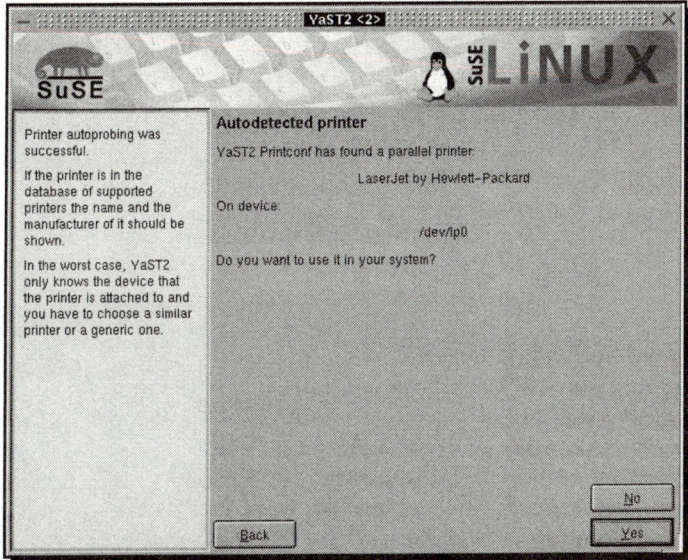

Fig. 4.10 The YaST2 Autodetection Screen

Pressing the **Yes** button, displays in the next configuration screen a default printer name as 'Printer1', which you can change. We selected to call our printer by its correct name (for purposes of identification), but you must not include spaces in the name; use instead the underscore character. We selected to call our printer by the name HP_LaseJet_5M.

Next, the configuration process displays the current printer settings with current paper size, etc. Pressing the **Next** button, displays the last configuration screen which can be used to choose the printer you have from the displayed list, and add another printer. Having made your selection, press the **Finish** button. A confirmation box will be displayed telling you that your printer has been successfully configured.

Configuring your Modem

Normally, your modem is configured automatically by the SuSE Linux Installer. However, if that is not the case or you have changed your modem, then follow the procedure below.

Change to user 'root', as discussed earlier on in this chapter, then start YaST2 by left-clicking the SuSE Work Menu icon on the KPanel, shown here, then on the pop-up menu (see Fig. 4.8) click on the **configuration with YaST2** option. This displays the YaST2 System Configuration screen shown in Fig. 4.11, with the **Network/Modem+ISDN** option selected.

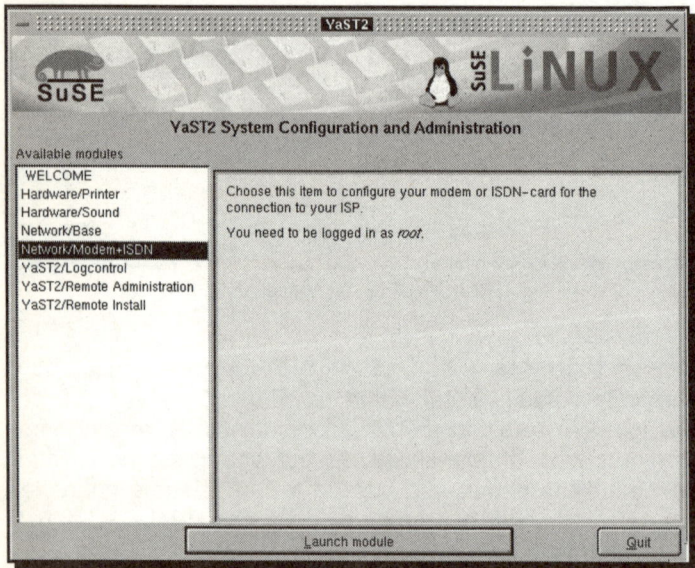

Fig. 4.11 The YaST2 System Configuration Screen

Pressing the **Launch module** bar at the bottom of the System Configuration screen, autodetects your modem using a procedure similar to the one used with the printer configuration discussed in the previous section.

Configuring your Dial-up Connection

Before you can connect to your Internet Service Provider (ISP), you need to configure your dial-up connection, as follows:

- Left-click the **K Start** button and select **KPanel, Add Applications, Internet, Kppp** option from the cascade menus, as shown below in Fig. 4.12.

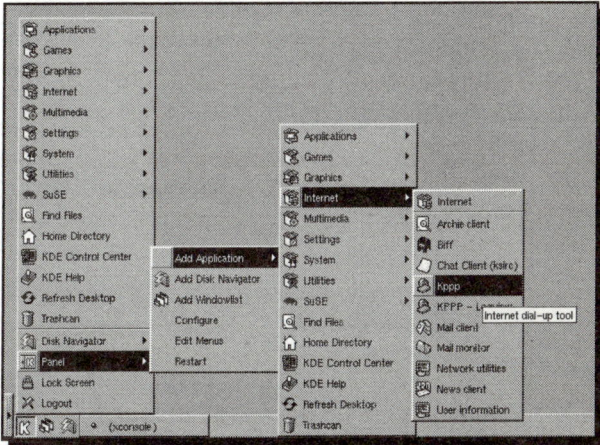

Fig. 4.12 Starting the Internet Dial-up Configuration

- On the displayed dialogue box (Fig. 4.13), press the **Setup** button.

Fig. 4.13 The Kppp Dialogue Box

- This opens up the kppp Configuration dialogue box with several tabs at its top, as shown below in Fig. 4.14.

Fig. 4.14 The Kppp Configuration Dialogue Box

- With the Accounts tab selected, press the **New** button which displays the New Account dialogue box, shown on the next page in Fig. 4.15, in which you enter your ISP's details, such as Name and Telephone number. The information on the dialogue boxes of the other tabs of Fig. 4.14 has already been entered by the system when the modem was configured, except for the information on the DNS tab dialogue box, which you will have to enter yourself.

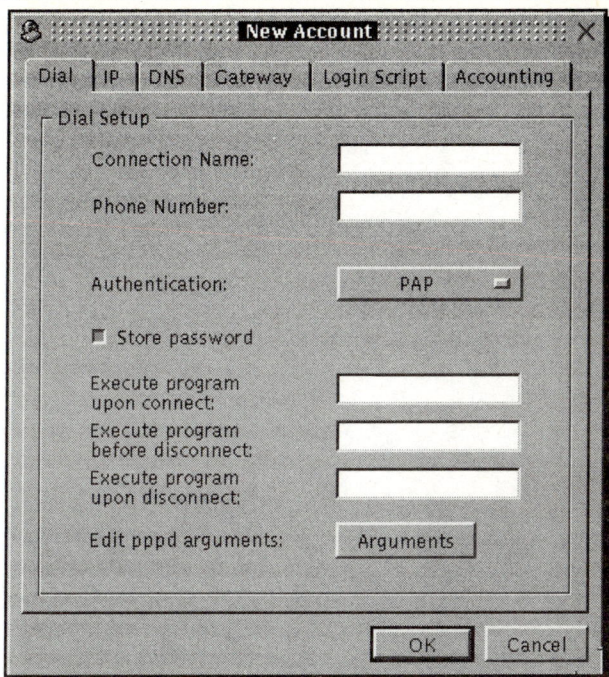

Fig. 4.15 The New Account Dialogue Box

• Having entered the appropriate information in the 'Connection Name' and 'Phone Number' fields, click the DNS tab to display the dialogue box shown on the next page (Fig. 4.16). In this box, type the 'Domain Name' of your ISP and their 'DNS IP Address' (if you do not know either of these, then contact your ISP for the relevant information - without this information, you will not be able to surf the Internet or send and receive e-mail). The information we show on our screen dump is made up and of no use to you.

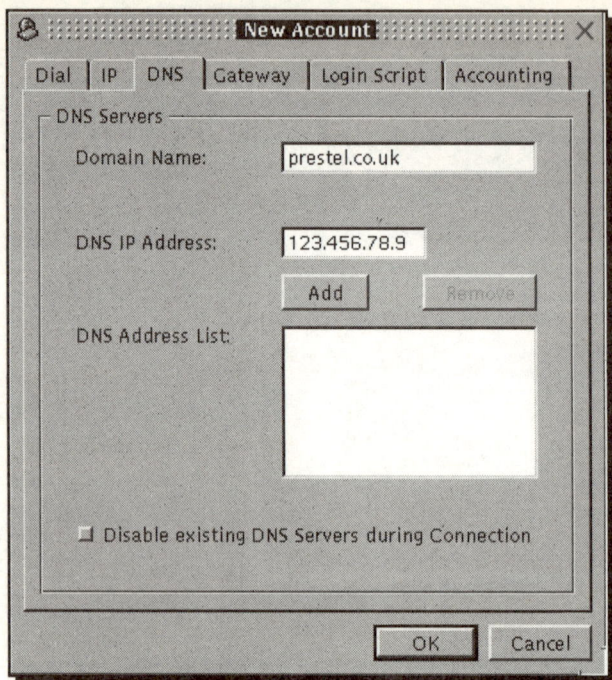

Fig. 4.16 The New Account Dialogue Box

- Next, press the **Add** button on the above dialogue box, then press the **OK** button on this and the next dialogue box. This causes the kppp dial-up connection box to open on your screen (similar to that of Fig. 4.13, but with the name of your ISP showing. You must now enter your 'login ID' and 'Password' before pressing the **Connect** button, which initialises your modem which starts ringing your ISP's telephone number.

Finally, the system adds the icon, shown to the left, on the KPanel so that you can invoke the Dial-up connection in the future by left-clicking it.

To test your system, press the **Connect** button on the kppp
dialogue box, shown below in Fig. 4.17.

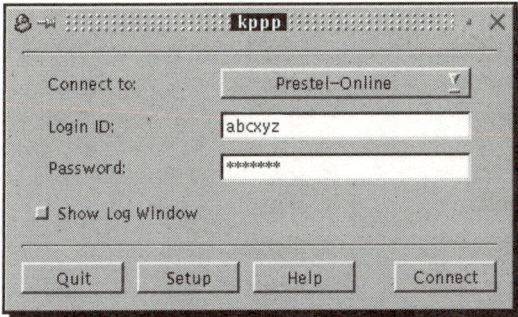

Fig. 4.17 Using kppp to Connect to an ISP

Once the connection has been made and the kppp box
iconifies on the Taskbar, click the Netscape icon on the
desktop and type www.suse.com in the **Location** box (see
next chapter). A screen similar to the one below should
display.

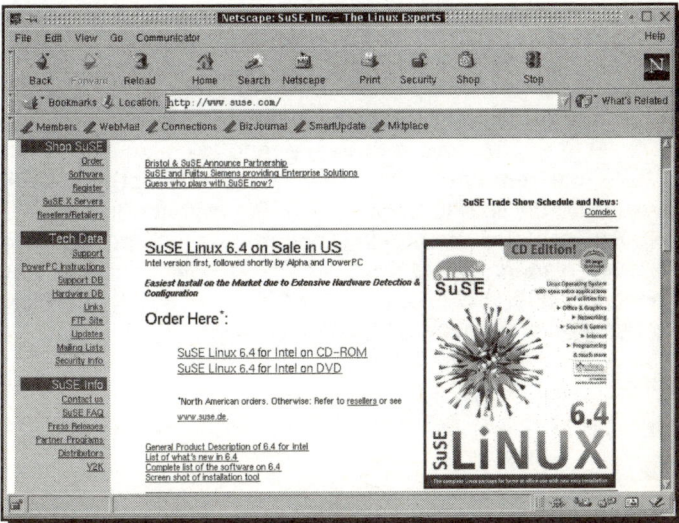

Fig. 4.18 Browsing the Internet with Netscape

We suggest you spend some time here browsing through the SuSE Web site. There is a lot of useful information to be found which will help you to understand a bit more about this distribution of Linux.

Once you have finished looking at the SuSE Web site, you can disconnect from the Internet, but first close Netscape, then click on the iconified kppp application on the Task bar, shown to the left, which displays the kppp disconnection box, shown below in Fig. 4.19.

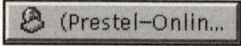

Fig. 4.19 Disconnecting from the ISP

As you can see, you are given information on what time you were connected to the Internet, and for how long you have remained connected.

Ideally what we would like to be able to do is to have the connection to the Internet made automatically whenever we ask Netscape to retrieve a Web site, and to disconnect when the link has remained idle for a specified length of time. However, to be able to achieve this, you will need to write a script that contains the required commands, and as we have not covered script writing, we will persevere with the dual way of connection; first connect to your ISP, then start Netscape. It is less painful than the alternative!

5

Netscape Program Features

Configuring Netscape

To start the Netscape Navigator, left-click the Netscape icon on the Desktop, which displays the following screen.

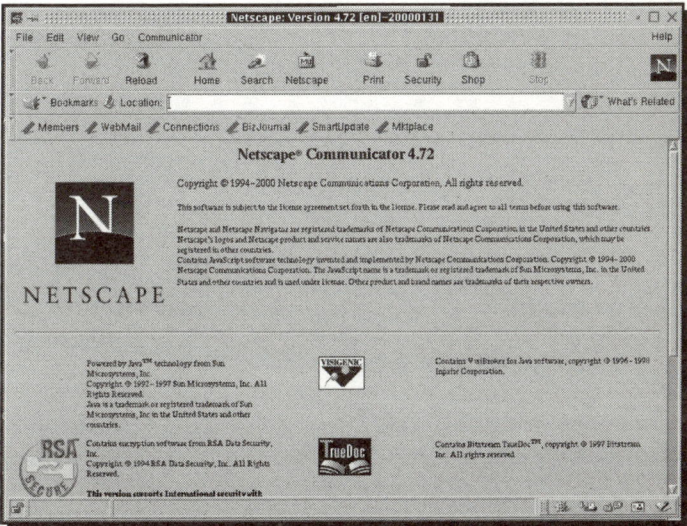

Fig. 5.1 Netscape Initial Screen

What we would like to do next is use the **Edit, Preferences** command to configure Netscape. However, as soon as you click on the **Edit** menu command, Netscape clears the above screen and loads a Web page from your hard disc (copied there during installation). Don't let this worry you.

Now using the **Edit, Preferences** command, opens up the Preferences dialogue box shown below in Fig. 5.2.

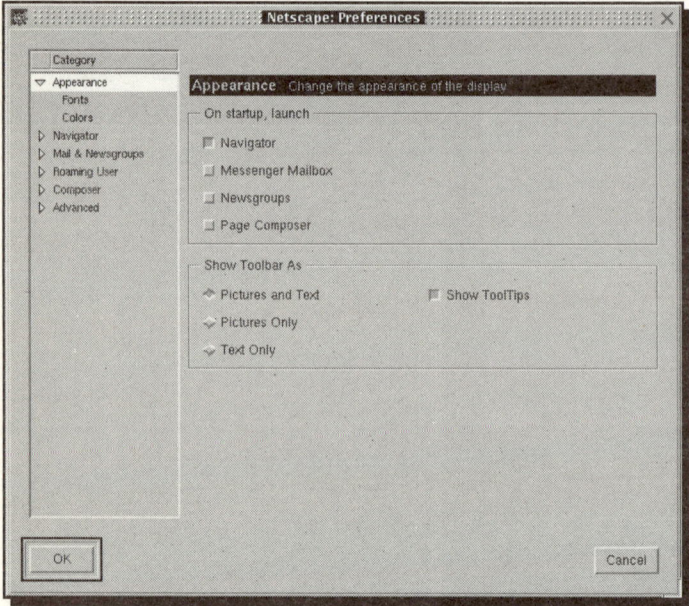

Fig. 5.2 Netscape Preferences Screen

From within this dialogue box, you can configure Netscape to your requirements. For example, you can select each item in the list under the **Category** option in turn to change the appearance of the display at start-up by selecting to launch one of four different screens: Navigator, Messenger Mailbox, Newsgroups, or Page Composer, with Navigator being the default selection. Which start-up screen you choose depends on your usage, although we suggest you stick with the default option (Navigator), as all the other options can be accessed from it and we can use it to configure Netscape for e-mail.

The next item on the list under **Category** is **Navigator**, which when selected, displays the screen of Fig. 5.3.

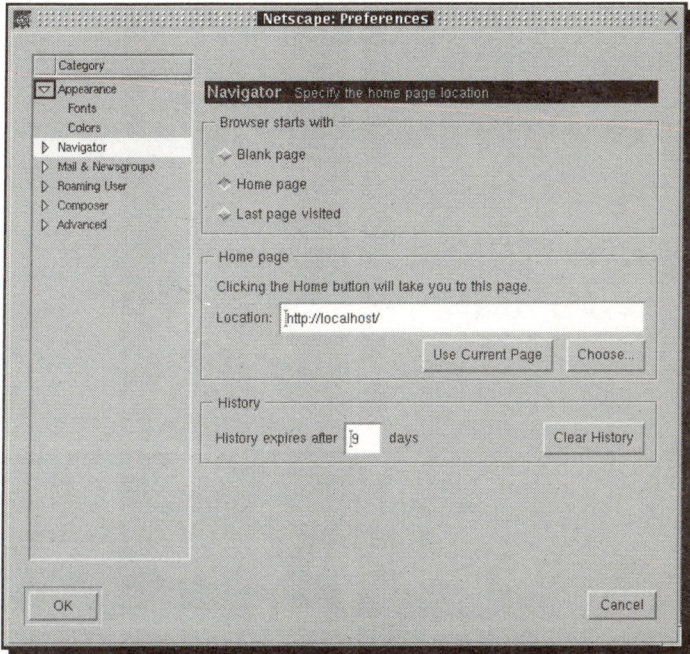

Fig. 5.3 Netscape Home Page Selection

Note that on the right panel of the above screen, under the **Browser starts with** preference, the Home page button is depressed. This causes Netscape to try to connect to the site given in the **Location** box. You can change the selected site within this box by typing in your preference, or you could even select to display a blank location page on start-up. If you make any changes to this dialogue box, do remember to click the **OK** button so that they can take effect - you might have to move the dialogue box upwards on your screen until the button is visible; this depends on your monitor settings. If you can not see this button, it must be because you have re-sized the window, but in fact you have only re-sized its frame!

The Navigator Screen

The screen dump of Fig. 5.4 below displays a blank page so that you can clearly see the screen annotation. To do this, we first selected to display a 'Blank page' on the **Browser starts with** field of the Netscape Preferences screen (see Fig. 5.3), then we closed and restarted the Netscape Navigator. These actions cause the display of the screen shown in Fig. 5.1, but clicking anywhere on the screen clears the message about Netscape and displays an empty screen.

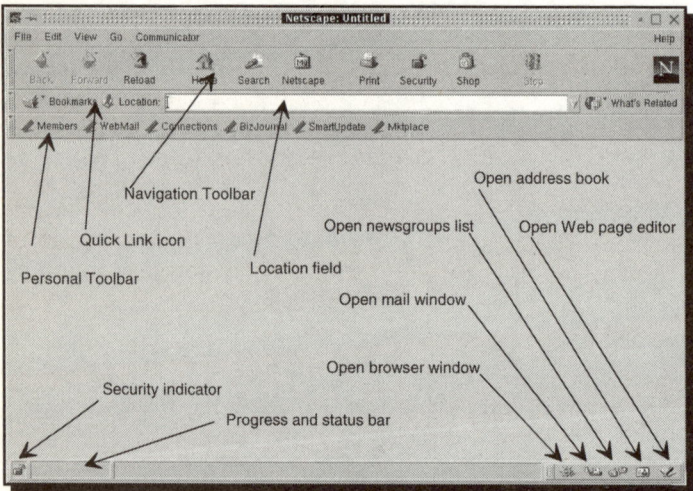

Fig. 5.4 Netscape Screen with Empty Window

It is perhaps worth spending some time examining the various parts that make up this Navigator window. Just as any other graphical Linux application, the Navigator follows the usual convention of displaying a window control button, pin button, title and menu bars, and the three buttons at the top right of the display that control the window (for a detailed description of these, see page 30). However, unlike the Terminal Emulator window, the above screen displays additional areas with the following functions:

Area	*Function*
Navigation toolbar	A bar of icons that you click to carry out some of the more common navigation actions in Netscape.
Quick Link icon	The chain link icon you drag onto the Bookmarks button to create a new Bookmark. You need to click the Bookmarks button and use the **File, Bookmark** command for this to take effect.
Location field	Shows the location of the current page, or the URL of a new page to Go To next. A list of recently visited locations can be opened by clicking the down-arrow small button to the right of the Location text box.
Personal toolbar	Clicking the buttons on this toolbar automatically loads on-line pages of information to help you find your way around the Web.
Status indicator	Shows the data transfer rate in percentage terms.
Page display	The main body of the window that displays Web pages.
Security indicator	The key symbol that shows if a document is secure. The broken key, as shown, indicates that it is insecure. A solid key indicates that it is secure.
Status bar	The animated bar that shows the progress of a downloading operation, the URL address of the link or graphic, pointed to by the mouse, or the function of a screen item pointed to by the mouse.
Browser icon	The icon you click to open a browser window.

Mail icon	The envelope icon that you click to open an e-mail window.
Newsgroups icon	The icon you click to open the list of available newsgroups.
Address book	The icon you click to open an address book window which can be used to enter, edit, or search for e-mail addresses of your contacts.
Web page editor	The icon you click to open up a Web page editor window in which you can load a specified Web page in order to edit it, then either save it on your hard disc or publish it on the Web.

The Navigation Toolbar

Most Linux applications are now fully equipped with a Toolbar option, and Netscape is no exception, as shown below. Netscape calls this the Navigation Toolbar and contains a series of buttons that you can click with your mouse pointer to quickly carry out certain navigation functions.

The functions of these buttons are pretty self-explanatory. Clicking on them produces the following actions:

Button	*Function*
Back	Displays the previous page in the history list.
Forward	Displays the next page in the history list.
Reload	Brings a fresh copy of the current Netscape page to the viewer. This is rapidly brought from the cache, unless the page has changed, in which case it is downloaded from source.

Home	Displays your specified home page, with the SuSE home page as the default.
Search	Lets you specify a word or phrase to locate within the current Web page.
Netscape	Displays the Netscape Home page (see Fig. 5.5).
Print	Prints the contents of the currently displayed Web page.
Security	Lets you select the security level.
Shop	Connects you the SuSE Shop Home page.
Stop	Stops downloading information.

If you find the Toolbar buttons, or the buttons on the other two bars too intimidating, you can change the way they appear on your screen, or remove them altogether, by clicking the Toggle switch to the left of each bar. To display them in their former position, click the Toggle switch once more.

The Location/Go To Field

The location field shows you the location (or URL address) of the current page being viewed. If you know the URL of the next page you want to look at, you can type it into this field and the label will change to **Go To,** as shown below.

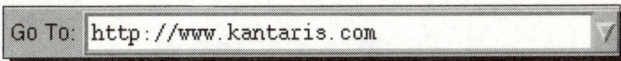

Go To: http://www.kantaris.com

Simply pressing the <Enter> key will load the page and the label will change back to **Location**.

A pull-down menu, opened by clicking the down arrow at the right of the field, lets you choose from the 10 most recent locations you have entered. This can save some typing!

The Personal Toolbar

Under the Location field there is another toolbar, which you will probably disable very soon after you get used to the Navigator and the Web. These are the Personal toolbar buttons shown below.

These buttons open various on-line pages prepared for you by Netscape and kept at their site. They are well worth exploring and may give you some ideas about where to go on the Web, and indeed, what can be usefully achieved instead of just surfing aimlessly from one link to another.

Below, we show what displays when you click the Netscape icon on the Navigation toolbar, provided you are connected to the Internet! What appears below is what was displayed the last time we visited Netscape's site. This will almost certainly have changed by the time you try it!

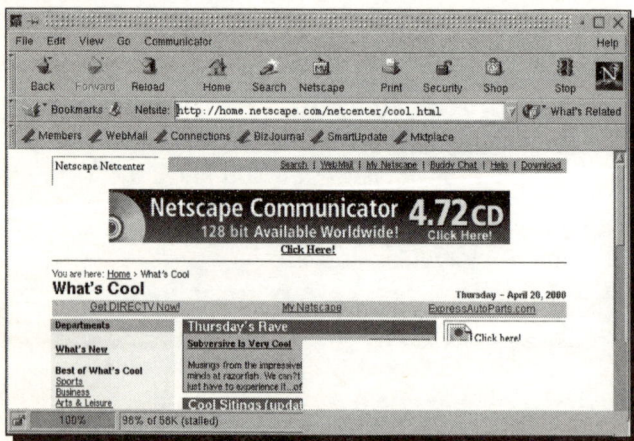

Fig. 5.5 The Netscape Home Page

The underlined words on this screen are in fact links, some of them to the same site, others to different sites. On screen, such links are blue and underlined, and each one almost certainly has many more links built into it.

Your Own Home Page

When you browse the World Wide Web you'll see the term 'home page' used quite a lot. The home page is usually the starting point, or starting page, of a Web site, which gives an overview of what you'll find at the site.

Your own home page is the Web page that Netscape Navigator automatically opens when you first switch on. By default, your browser is set to open at SuSE's own home page site, which is on a computer in Germany. This may be useful to you at the beginning, particularly as you can browse their help database, but you might want to change it later on. This, like most things in Netscape, is quite easy to do, as we explained on page 59. You can select the address of your favourite Web page, or the file, that you want to see every time Netscape starts. The file can be located on your hard disc, but must be of a type that is readable by the Navigator.

Following are some ideas for a home page:

- Some people make up their own home page of data and links to their favourite starting points.

- Others use one of the many search engine pages available on the Web, but unless you use a local one, this can sometimes be slow.

- If you are connected to a company, or work, network they should have a home page that can show useful internal information and links.

- You could use your Internet Service Provider's own home page, or Netscape's home page.

Remember that wherever you are on the Web, clicking the **Home** Toolbar icon, will return you to your home page.

*****

If you want to get to grips with the Internet in general and how to use Netscape to surf the Web, and use the program's very powerful e-mail features in particular, may we suggest you have a look at one of our books *Using Netscape on the Internet* (BP415), also published by Bernard Babani Books.

Configuring Netscape for E-mail

To configure Netscape so that you can send and receive electronic mail, left click the 'Open the mail window and get new messages' icon, shown here, and to be found at the bottom of the Netscape screen. This displays the screen below, Fig. 5.6.

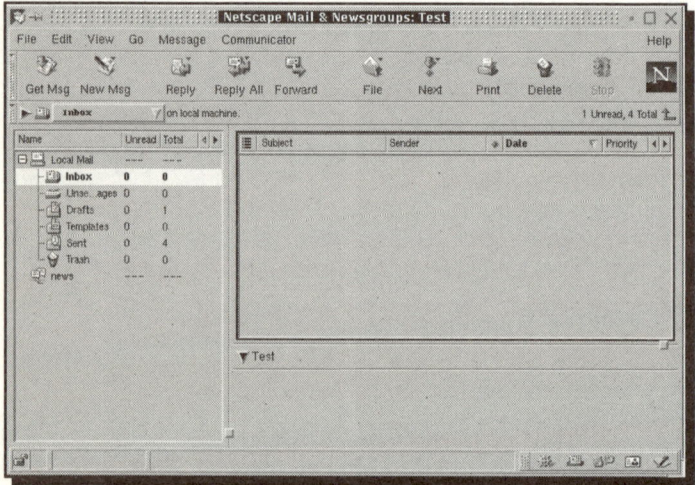

Fig. 5.6 Netscape Mail & Newsgroups Screen

Next, select the **Edit, Preferences** menu option which now opens a slightly different Preferences dialogue box, which has a lot more options under the **Mail & Newsgroups** category, than those available in Fig. 5.3.

To configure Netscape for e-mail, you must fill in the **Identity** panel, shown on the next page in Fig. 5.7, but with your own details. In fact, from here on, you will need certain information from your ISP, so that you can also fill in the information required in the **Mail Servers** panel, also shown on the next page in Fig. 5.8. To fill in the entry under Incoming Mail Servers in this last screen, you need to highlight the default entry already there, then press the **Edit** button and fill in the dialogue box of Fig. 5.9.

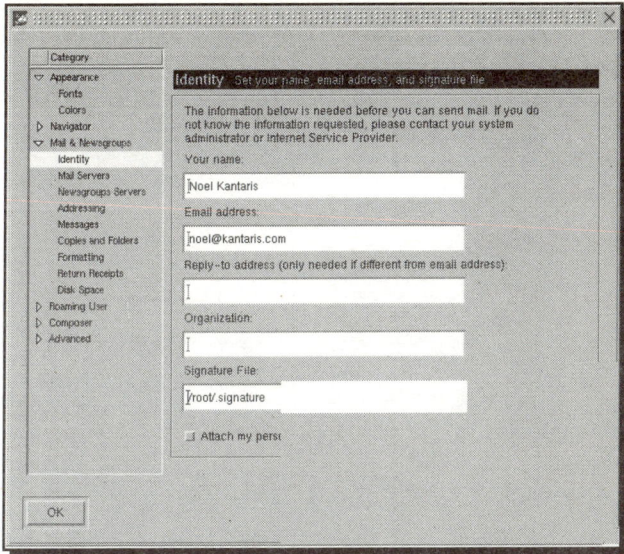

Fig. 5.7 Netscape Identity Preference Screen

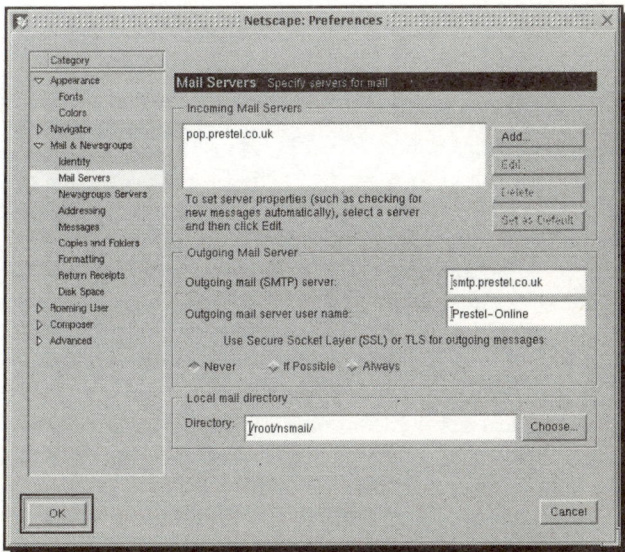

Fig. 5.8 Netscape Mail Servers Preference Screen

As we have already mentioned, the information under Incoming Mail Servers in Fig. 5.8, is obtained by filling in the dialogue box below.

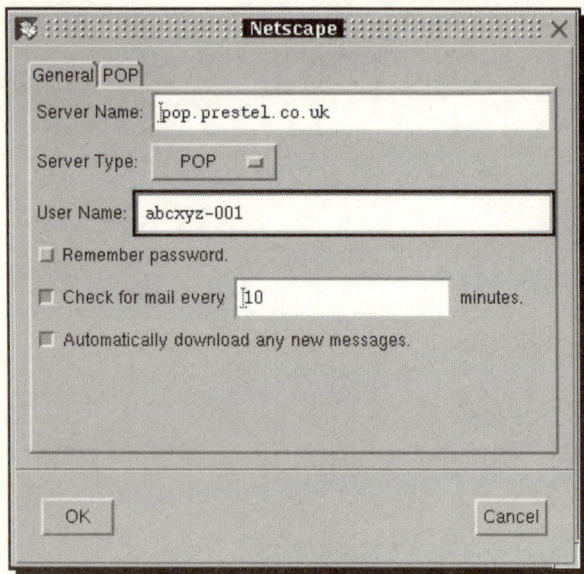

Fig. 5.9 Configuring the Incoming Mail Servers

Again, as you can see, you need to know some rather specific information for your ISP without which you will not be able to use the e-mail facility. In the screen dump above, we show sufficient authentic information to guide you through your task. Although our ISP is **prestel.co.uk**, yours will most likely be different. Other sensitive information in these last three dialogue boxes has been changed slightly, but still gives you a very good idea of what is required on your part.

Note: If you are connected to the Internet via a modem, click the 'Check for mail every ... minutes' button to disable this facility which will stop Netscape attempting to fetch mail when you are working off-line, and producing the annoying error messages. You will also need to select to display a blank location page on start-up (see Fig. 5.3).

Testing the E-mail Facility

The best way to check that your e-mail facility works, is to compose a short e-mail message and send it to yourself. If you receive it back a few minutes later, then all is well. To start the process, click the New Message icon , shown here, and found on the Toolbar of the Mail & Newsgroups screen, and type a short message in the displayed Composer screen, shown below.

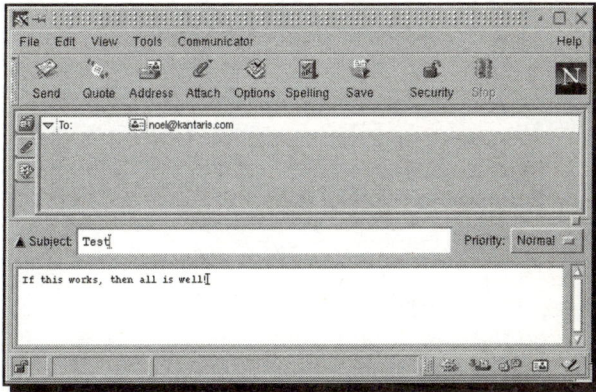

Fig. 5.10 Composing an E-mail

Note: You need to fill in the address of the person to whom you intend to send your message in the **To:** text box, a suitable short description of what the message is all about in the **Subject:** text box, and the actual message in the main text box.

Next, and before you click the Send icon on the Toolbar, connect to your ISP by activating the Internet dial-up tool, and once connected, press the Send icon. If all is well, your message is sent, and your display reverts to the Mail & Newsgroups screen (see Fig. 5.6). After a minute or so, check if you have new mail by pressing the Get Msg icon on the Mail & Newsgroups screen. If you have mail, you will be informed, as shown in Fig. 5.11.

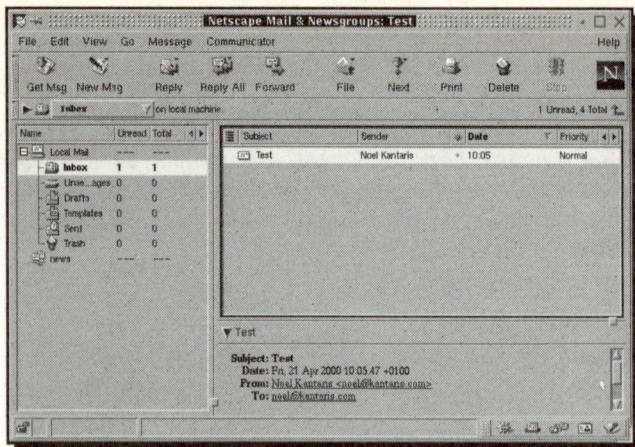

Fig. 5.11 Netscape Mail & Newsgroups Screen

Double-clicking on the received message, opens it up for you to read. If you find that the font size in your e-mail is too small to read clearly, then use the **Edit, Preferences** command and select the **Fonts** option under **Appearance**, where you can change the size of your letters and whether they should appear mono spaced or not.

If you have written any e-mail messages and you have not sent them yet, trying to close the Mail & Newsgroups window displays the warning box shown here. Don't worry though, e-mail messages you have prepared but not sent, are save on disc and will still be there next time you start your e-mail facility. Information on this is shown on the Mail & Newsgroups screen against the title 'Unse ... ages'. The size of the box is not long enough to hold the full caption which is, of course, 'Unsent Messages'.

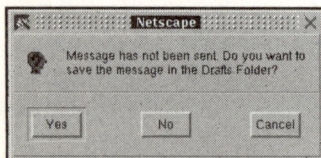

Note: The icons on the Toolbar of the various screens dealing with e-mail, change to suit the type of operation you are carrying out at the time, which is only to be expected.

6

The KDE File Manager

Configuring the Kᴀᴍ Application

The way you can activate the K File Manager (kfm) depends on whether you have logged in as 'root', or you have logged in as an ordinary user. These are as follows:

(i) If you have logged in as 'root', then you can either access kfm via the **K Start, System, File manager** cascade menu, or by clicking the 'Home folder' icon on the KPanel, shown here to the right.

(ii) If you have logged in as an ordinary user, then you can only access kfm via the 'Home folder' icon.

Whichever way you choose to start kfm as 'root', the first time you access it, it will display your folders and files (to be explained shortly) in its default mode, as follows:

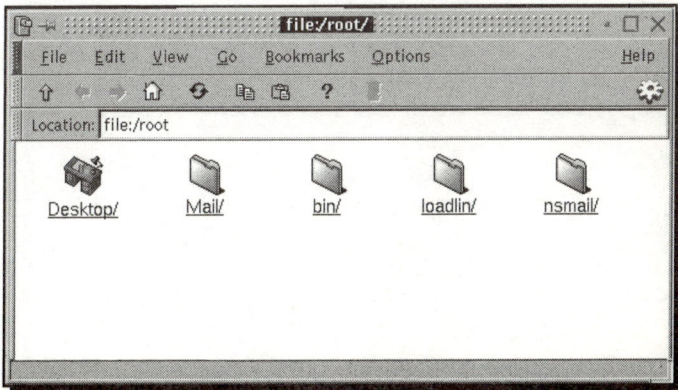

Fig. 6.1 The KFM Default File and Folder Display

However, you can control what is displayed on your screen by using the **View** sub-menu. For example, you might choose to display the 'tree' (the way folders and files are structured on your hard disc) on the left panel of the kfm window, as shown below in Fig. 6.2, or to actually change the way folders

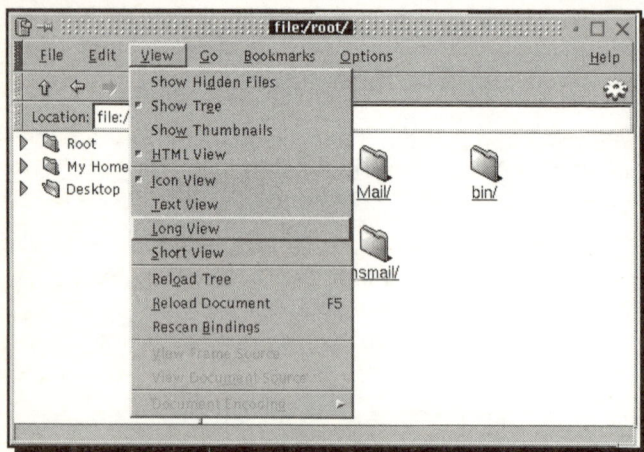

Fig. 6.2 Selecting how to View the KFM Window

and files are depicted by choosing **Long View** from the **View** sub-menu. Your display then changes to:

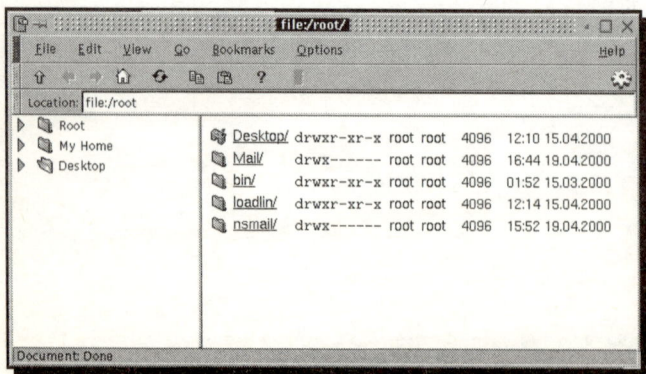

Fig. 6.3 The Tree and Long File KFM Display for 'root'

We find the way that folders and files are displayed in Fig. 6.3 preferable to the default way. For a start, one can see the folder/file permissions (whether it is read only, read and write, or whatever), its size in bytes, and the time and date it was created. Such information can be very useful at times.

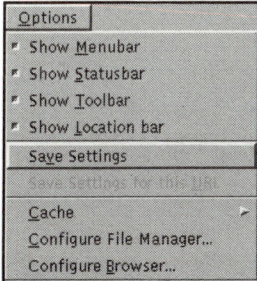

Fig. 6.4 Saving KFM Settings

Having selected a preferred way of viewing your folders and files, and/or the display of the 'tree' structure alongside it, you can make this preference permanent by choosing the sub-menu **Save Settings** from the **Options** menu, as shown to the left in Fig. 6.4. All that will happen is that next time you use the kfm application, it will display in your selected way, rather than the default, but you can change this at any time.

If you logged in as an ordinary user (in our case below as noelkan), then what is displayed (after going through the same **View** preferences), is slightly different from logging in as 'root', as can be seen below in Fig. 6.5.

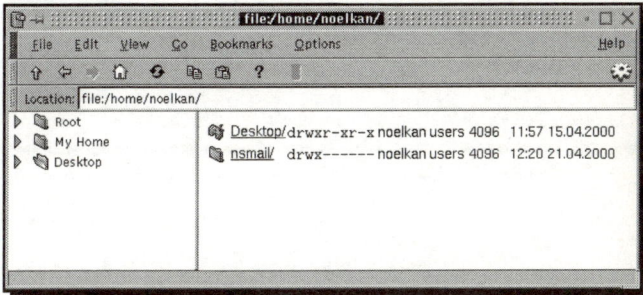

Fig. 6.5 The KFM File Structure of an Ordinary User

At this stage, we ask you to note the respective 'locations' for 'root' and 'noelkan' in Fig. 6.3 & 6.5, which are file:/root and file:/home/noelkan, respectively.

The Linux File Structure

As you can see from the screen dumps of Fig. 6.3 & 6.5, in Linux the file structure is unified with everything growing under the root (/) directory or folder (don't confuse that with the super user 'root'). For example, the 'location' for both screen dumps starts with file:/, then below that, if you have logged in as 'root', the word *root* is shown, but if you have logged in as, say, noelkan, then *home/noelkan* is shown. This file structure can be shown diagrammatically (in an oversimplified form), as follows:

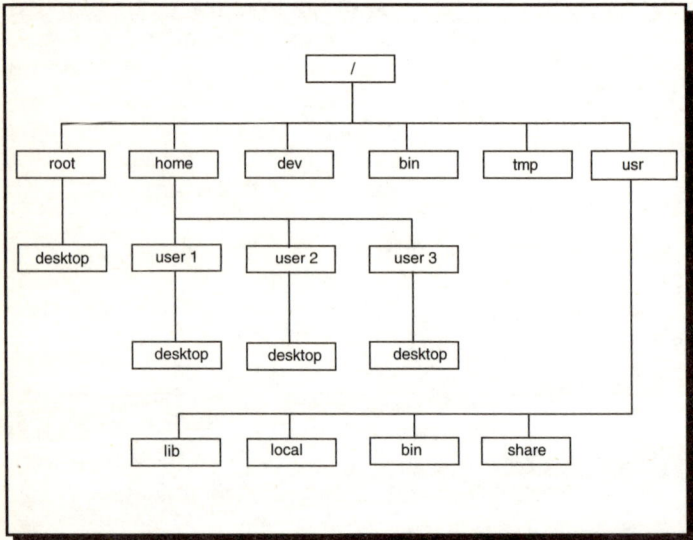

Fig. 6.6 The Linux File Structure - Simplified

Each ordinary user has a common 'home' folder, while the super-user has 'root' as the home folder; the super-user can access all folders, including the 'home' folder of other users, as shown on the next page in Fig. 6.7. Each user, whether 'root' or ordinary, has their own desktop, but ordinary users can only access their own folders, shared utilities and program applications.

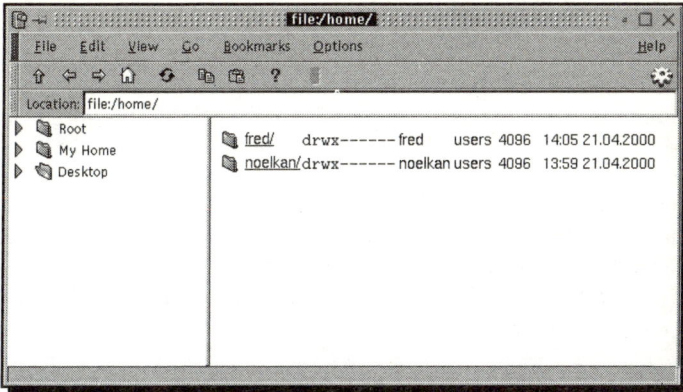

Fig. 6.7 Super-User's Access of Other Users' Home Directory

Unlike Microsoft Windows where the file structure is centred on drive names or letters, Linux deals in mount points, to be discussed in the next section. For example, 'root' and system files could be on one hard drive while other users and shared applications could be on a different drive. Linux does not care how many drives or partitions are in use, provided it is possible to 'mount' such drives, in which case all users, system files and shared applications appear under the root (/) directory or folder.

This makes for a very unified and flexible system, while Windows is totally inflexible by comparison - try moving a Windows application from one drive to another (better still, don't bother). In Windows you will have to reinstall such applications, while in Linux you don't have such problems.

In a Linux file structure, such as the one described above, where the 'root' folder and system files are on a separate hard disc (or partition) from that of the 'home' folder and shared applications, you could quite easily go as far as to format the drive (or partition) where 'root' is to be found, then install a different Linux distribution in that drive (or partition), without affecting the other users' personal files. Pretty impressive you must admit!

Mounting and Dismounting File Systems

The Linux file system, as we have seen in the previous section, does not deal in hard drive names or letters, but in mount points. In other words, you can use any number of drives or partitions, including drives attached to a network or drives formatted under MS-DOS, provided you can mount them. As an example, we show below the command you must type in the KDE terminal emulator to mount an external SCSI removable hard drive which was formatted under MS-DOS, but detected by Linux during installation.

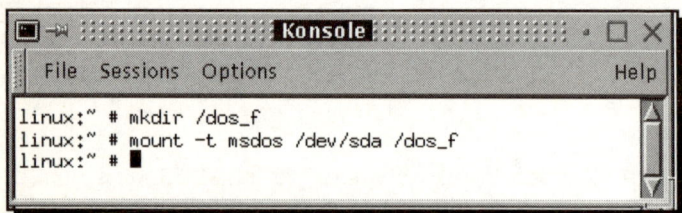

```
linux:~ # mkdir /dos_f
linux:~ # mount -t msdos /dev/sda /dos_f
linux:~ # █
```

Fig. 6.8 Mounting an External MS-DOS SCSI Hard Drive

The first line of the two-line command in Fig. 6.8, allows 'root' to make a directory or folder (mkdir) immediately under root (/), called dos_f. This command is needed only the first time you use this system, because the directory /dos_f must exist before you issue the second command which mounts the drive. At all subsequent Linux sessions, you only need to issue the second command line in Fig. 6.8 to mount this external hard drive so that you can access all the files on it, be it files created under Linux or MS-DOS. To prove that the drive is mounted, type in the command

    ls /dos_f

which should respond with a listing (ls) of all the files on the external hard drive.

To dismount such a drive you will have to issue the command:

    umount /dos_f

which stands for 'unmount', but without the 'n'.

Common Linux File Commands

A summary of the most common Linux commands is given below - optional arguments in a command are shown in [ ].

Command	*Description / Action*
cd dir	Changes to subdirectory 'dir'.
cd ..	Changes to parent directory
cd /dir	Changes to directory '/dir'.
cd	Changes to user's home directory.
cp file1 file2	Copies source 'file1' to destination 'file2'.
ln [-s] source link_nam	Creates a [symbolic link] 'link_nam' in the currently logged directory to 'source'. 'Link_nam' defines the path where the required file or directory is to be found.
ls	Lists contents of the currently logged directory.
ls dir	Lists contents of 'dir'.
ls -l [dir]	Lists contents of 'dir' in detail.
ls -a [dir]	Lists contents of 'dir', including hidden files.
mkdir new_dir	Creates the new directory or folder 'new_dir'.
mv file1 file2	Moves or renames 'file1' to 'file2'.
rm file	Removes (deletes) 'file'.
rm -r direct	Removes (deletes) 'direct' recursively.
rmdir direct	Removes (deletes) 'direct', but only if it is empty.

Using KFM to Action Linux Commands

Most Linux commands listed in the previous section can also
be accessed by using shortcut menus. For example, if you
wanted to create a sub-directory or folder under an existing
one, left-lick the parent folder to select it, then right-click to
obtain the following shortcut menu:

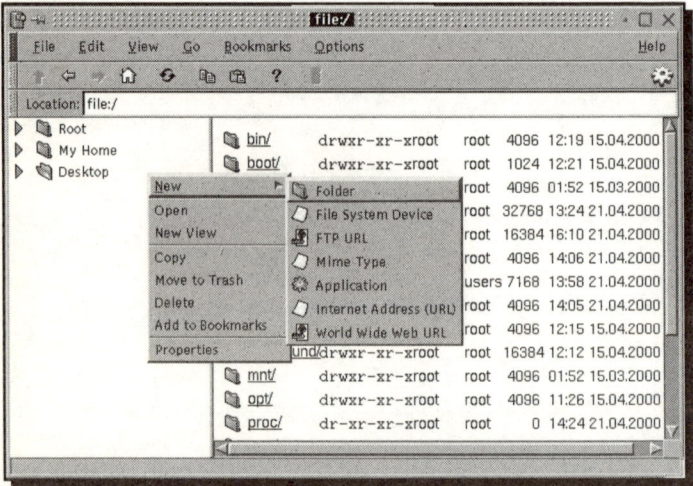

Fig. 6.9 Creating a New Folder Using KFM Shortcut Menus

Fig. 6.10 New Folder Dialogue Box

Selecting the **New,
Folder** command, opens
up a dialogue box for
you to type in the name
for your new folder, as
shown in Fig. 6.10.

Both files and folders can be manipulated equally well using
shortcut menus within kfm, as shown in the left shortcut
menu in Fig. 6.9 above. From this menu, amongst other
things, you can Copy, Move to Trash and Delete files and
folders, or look at their Properties.

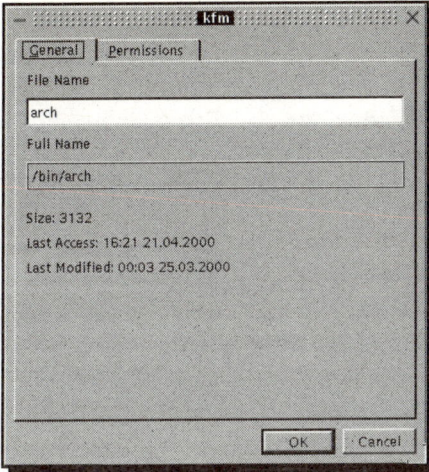

Fig. 6.11 The General File Properties
Dialogue Box

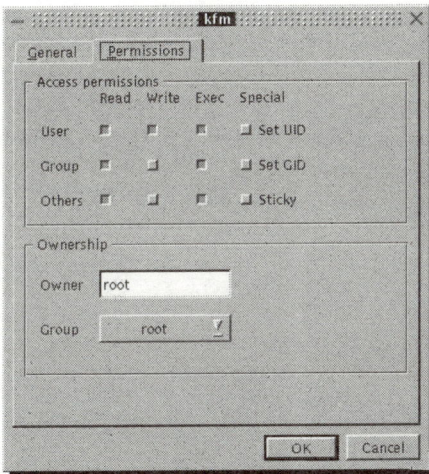

Fig. 6.12 The Permissions File Properties
Dialogue Box

The screen shown here in Fig. 6.11, displays the Properties box of a file called **arch** which is to be found in the **/bin** folder, as you can see when the General tab is pressed. You can also see the size of the file, when it was last accessed and when it was last modified.

If you now press the Permissions tab, you will see the display shown in Fig. 6.12. From here, you can access the file permissions for user, group and others, as well as the ownership of the file. Needless to say, you need to have logged in as 'root' to be able to change any of the permissions. If you logged in as an ordinary user, you will find that you can only change file per-missions of your own files, but with all other files these facilities are greyed out and inaccessible to you.

Using KFM to Surf the Internet

If you want to quickly visit a site on the Internet, you can always do it from the KDE file manager (kfm). You must have noticed by now, that as you navigate through the file system the address of the selected file or folder is always displayed in the Location box, near the top of the kfm window (see, for example, Fig. 6.9).

If, however, you now type the address of a Web site in the Location box instead of a file or folder, then kfm will locate and download that site's page, as shown below, provided you first connect to the Internet using the kppp, as we discussed in the previous chapter. Furthermore, kfm also supports bookmarks and is very fast.

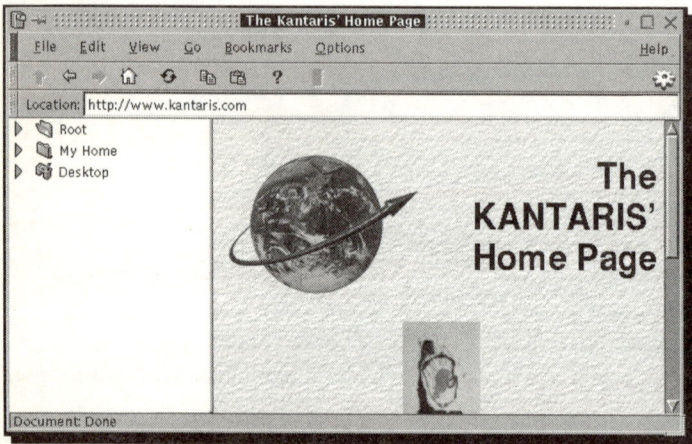

Fig. 6.13 Using KFM to Browse the Internet

As you will see for yourself, if you try it, the KDE file manager can locate Web sites quickly and efficiently, but admittedly not always perfectly. Nevertheless, it is a quick method of getting information from the Web and does not require the resources necessary when using Netscape.

Getting Help on KFM

We suggest you spend some time finding out for yourself the capabilities of kfm. One good starting point is the considerable Help System accessed from its Help menu, as shown below.

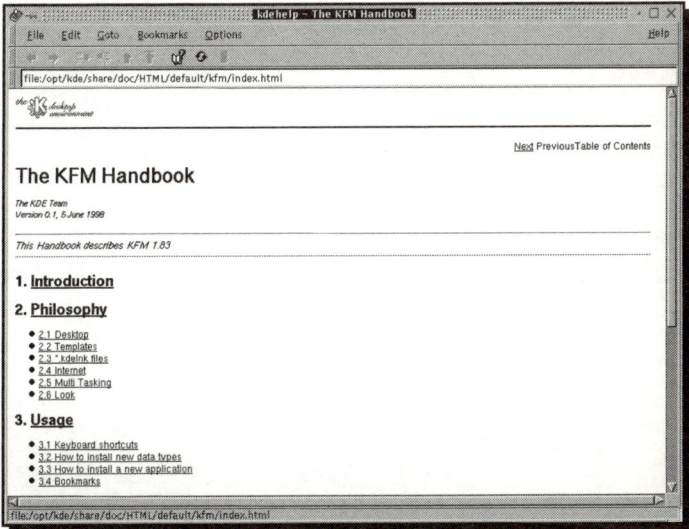

Fig. 6.14 Using KFM Help System

As you can see, there are quite a few topics to go through, so we leave it to you.

Note: We have discussed both methods of manipulating folders and files; using the KDE file manager kfm, or issuing Linux commands in a shell. These are supposed to complement each other - sometimes one method is easier that the other - so we suggest you explore both ways of using the various operations. However, we also suggest you login as an ordinary user when manipulating files - it is much safer this way!

7

Controlling Information

In this chapter we show you how to control information, whether this is in the form of text, or graphics. In particular, we will introduce you to the KEdit text editor, how to write scripts, and how to deal with graphics.

Linux's KEdit

When you are using Linux or one of its applications, you will invariably come across a **Readme.txt** file which contains last minute information not available in printed form in the User Guides. Vendors create such text files which can be read by the Text Editor Accessory, known as KEdit. What follows, will show you how to read such files, print them, or copy them onto the Clipboard, so that you can transfer the information into another package.

Although the KEdit text editor has no pagination or formatting features, it is a useful accessory for writing and reading simple documents. To access KEdit, click the **K Start** button, select **Applications, Text Editor**, then use the **File, Open** command on the displayed window, locate the file you would like to read, and left-click it.

Another way of opening text files is to first locate them using the kfm, then left-click the required file. If the file is indeed a text file, then KEdit is loaded, and the file in question is automatically opened. Obviously this is by far the simplest way of reading a text file. On the next page, we show you the result of using the kfm application to locate the file

```
/root/loadlin/initrd.txt
```

and then left-clicking it.

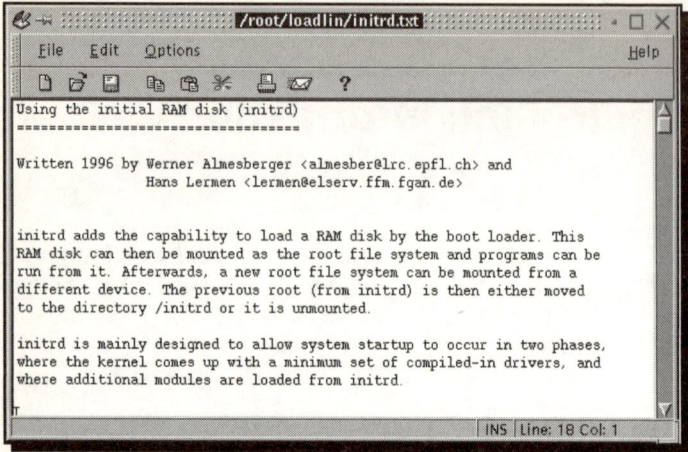

Fig. 7.1 Using KEdit to Open a Text File

Like all other Linux graphical applications (see Chapter 3, page 30), KEdit conforms to a common style window with a Title bar, Menu bar, and Toolbar, and with the Toolbar icons being mostly self-explanatory. If you have used a word processor you will find this editor extremely simple.

The KEdit Window

The top line of the KEdit window is the Title bar which contains the name of the displayed document, and if this bar is dragged with the mouse the window can be moved around the screen; you can also use the <Alt> key with the left mouse button pressed down within the window area to move it. Also, just like any other window, its size can be changed by dragging any of its four sides in the required direction.

The second line of the window displays the Menu bar which allows access to the following sub menus:

File   Edit   Options   Help

As described in Chapter 3 (page 34), the sub-menus are accessed by using the mouse to point to an option, then left clicking it to reveal the pull-down sub-menu of the activated menu option.

The KEdit Toolbar

As with most Linux graphical applications windows, the Toolbar contains a set of icon buttons that you click to carry out some of the more common menu functions. The actions of each icon are outlined on the screen dump below.

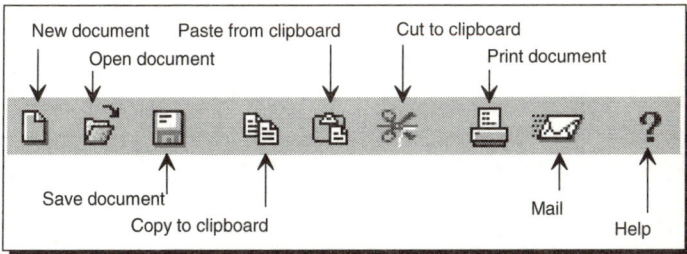

New document   Paste from clipboard   Cut to clipboard

Open document   Print document

Save document   Mail

Copy to clipboard   Help

Fig. 7.2 The KEdit Toolbar Icons

Opening a KEdit Document

In order to illustrate this section, either type in a short letter in a New document window, or open the initrd.txt file found in the /root/loadlin/ folder by left-clicking the Open button on KEdit's toolbar, shown here, which displays the following dialogue box.

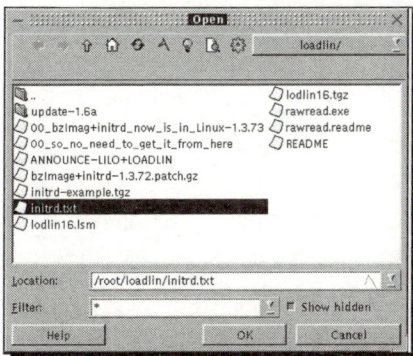

Fig. 7.3 The KEdit Open Dialogue Box

Note the browser type Toolbar icons at the top of the Open dialogue box. As you select a folder, its name is shown in the text box at the top right of the window, while the path to the selected file is displayed in the **Location** box at the bottom of the window. Finally, note that the file **Filter** is set to *, which means all files - there is no choice in selecting the type of file you would like to open.

Moving Around a KEdit Document

You can move the cursor around a document with the normal direction keys, as well as with the key combinations shown below.

To move	*Press*
Left one character	←
Right one character	→
Up one line	↑
Down one line	↓
To beginning of line	HOME or Ctrl+←
To end of line	END or Ctrl+→
Up one window	Page Up
Down one window	Page Down

Saving to a File

To save a document, click the Save toolbar icon, shown here, or use the **File, Save** command. An identical dialogue box to the Open dialogue box appears on the screen. You can select a folder, other than the one displayed, by clicking the 'Up to parent' icon on the toolbar and selecting a different folder.

Fig. 7.4 The KEdit Save As Dialogue Box

To save a document in the future with a different name use the **File, Save as** menu command.

Document Editing

For small deletions, such as letters or words, the easiest way is to use the <Delete> or <BkSp> keys. With the <Delete> key, position the cursor on the first letter you want to remove and press <Delete>; the letter is deleted and the following text moves one space to the left. With the <BkSp> key, position the cursor immediately to the right of the character to be deleted and press <BkSp>; the cursor moves one space to the left pulling the rest of the line with it and overwriting the character to be deleted. Note that the difference between the two is that with <Delete> the cursor does not move at all.

Text editing is usually carried out in the insert mode. Any characters typed will be inserted at the cursor location and the following text will be pushed to the right, and down. Pressing the <Insert> key will change to Overstrike mode, which causes entered text to overwrite any existing text at the cursor.

When larger scale editing is needed, use the **Cut, Copy** and **Paste** operations; the text to be altered must be 'selected' before the operation can be carried out. These functions are then available when the **Edit** sub-menu is activated, or Toolbar icons are used.

Selecting Text: The procedure in KEdit, is that before any operation such as editing can be carried out on text, you first select the text to be altered. Selected text is highlighted on the screen. This can be carried out in two ways:

  a. **Using the keyboard**; position the cursor on the first character to be selected, hold down the <Shift> key while using the direction keys to highlight the required text, then release the <Shift> key. Navigational key combinations can also be used with the <Shift> key to highlight blocks of text.

  b. **With the mouse**; click the left mouse button at the beginning of the block and drag the cursor across the block so that the desired text is highlighted, then release the mouse button.

Copying Blocks of Text: Once text has been selected it can be copied to another location in your present document, to another KEdit document, or to another Linux application. As with most of the editing operations there are many ways of doing this.

The first is by using the **Edit, Copy** command sequence from the menu, or clicking the Copy Toolbar icon, moving the cursor to the start of where you want the copied text, and using the **Edit, Paste** command, or clicking the Paste icon. Another method uses the quick key combinations, <Ctrl+C> to copy and <Ctrl+V> to paste.

To copy the same text again to another location in the document, move the cursor to the new location and paste it there with either of the above methods.

Moving Blocks of Text: Selected text can also be moved, in which case it is deleted in its original location. Use the **Edit, Cut,** command, or the <Ctrl+X> keyboard shortcut, or click the Cut icon, move the cursor to the required new location and then use the **Edit, Paste** command, <Ctrl+V>, or click the Paste icon. The moved text will be placed at the cursor location and will force any existing text to make room for it. This operation can be cancelled by simply pressing <Esc>.

Deleting Blocks of Text: When text is deleted it is removed from the document. With KEdit any selected text can be deleted by pressing **Edit, Cut,** or by simply pressing the <Delete> key. However, using **Edit, Cut** places the text on the Linux clipboard and allows you to use the **Edit, Paste** command, while using the <Delete> key, does not.

Finding and Replacing Text: KEdit allows you to search for specified text, or character combinations. In the 'Find' mode it will highlight each occurrence in turn so that you can carry out some action on it. In the 'Replace' mode you specify what replacement is to be carried out.

For example, in a long memo you may decide to replace every occurrence of the word 'disk' with the word 'disc'. This is very easy to do. First go to the beginning of the document, as searches operate in a forward direction by default, then choose the **Edit**, **Replace** command from KEdit's menu bar to open a dialogue box, like the one below.

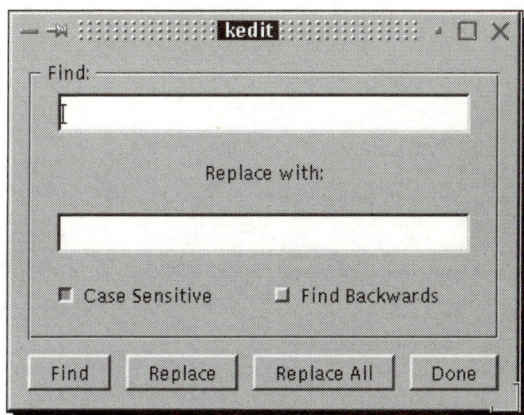

Fig. 7.5 The KEdit Replace Dialogue Box

You type what you want to search for in the **Find** box, then type the replacement word in the **Replace with** box. Next, you specify whether you want to find and replace words with the **Case Sensitive** option by check-marking the appropriate box. Finally, make a selection from one of the four buttons provided; selecting **Replace** requires you to manually confirm each replacement, whilst selecting **Replace All** will replace all occurrences of the word automatically.

Formatting a Document: As an example of formatting options, we show overleaf the Font Dialogue box which is displayed when you select the **Options, Font** menu command. Note, however, that although you can change the font type, font size, and have it display in bold and/or italic, such changes affect the whole document - there is no way to apply such formatting changes only to a part of the document.

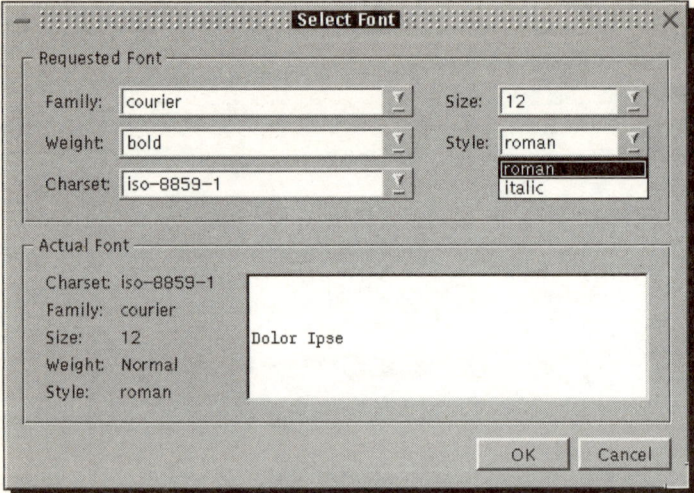

Fig. 7.6 The KEdit Select Font Dialogue Box

Date Stamping a Document: To date stamp a document, place the cursor where you want the current date and time to appear, then use the **Edit, Insert Date** menu command. The format of date stamping is shown below.

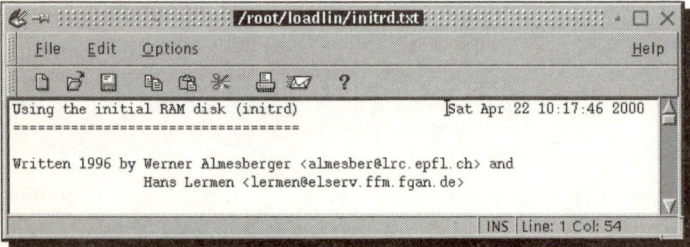

Fig. 7.7 Date Stamping a KEdit Document

Unfortunately, we could not find any way of changing the format of the date stamp to something shorter than the default.

Spell Checking a Document: A lot of information, whether in the form of a printed page, a 'readme' file, or an e-mail, appears these days full of errors and spelling mistakes. Some people do not seem to read their work before clicking the **Print**, **Save**, or **Send** button. With this version of KEdit this could be avoided, as the program supports spell checking.

To try out the KEdit Spell Checker, prepare a message in the New Document window, but make an obvious spelling mistake, maybe something similar to ours below. Then use the **Edit, Spellcheck** command to start the process.

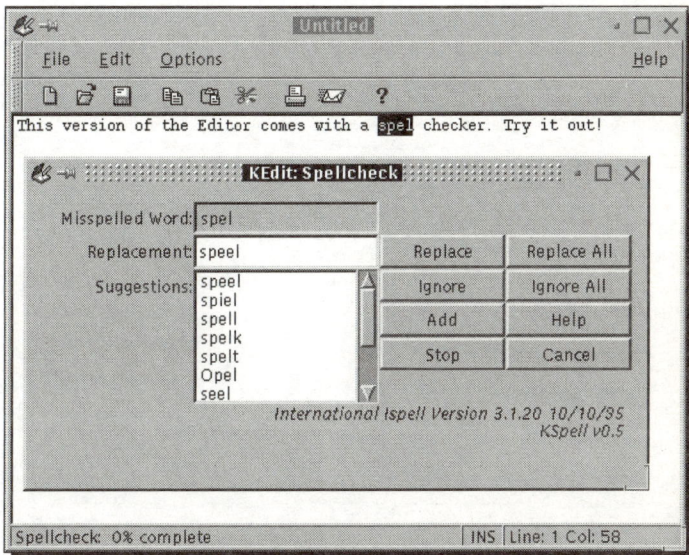

Fig. 7.8 Spell Checking a KEdit Document

Any words not recognised by the Spell Checker will be flagged up as above. If you are happy with the word, just click one of the **Ignore** buttons, otherwise you can either type a correction in the **Replacement** text box, or accept one of the words from the **Suggestions** list and then click the **Replace** button.

Printing Documents

As long as your printer has been properly installed and configured, you should have no problems printing your documents from the KEdit application. You can either use the **File, Print** menu command or click the Print icon on the KEdit Toolbar, shown to the left.

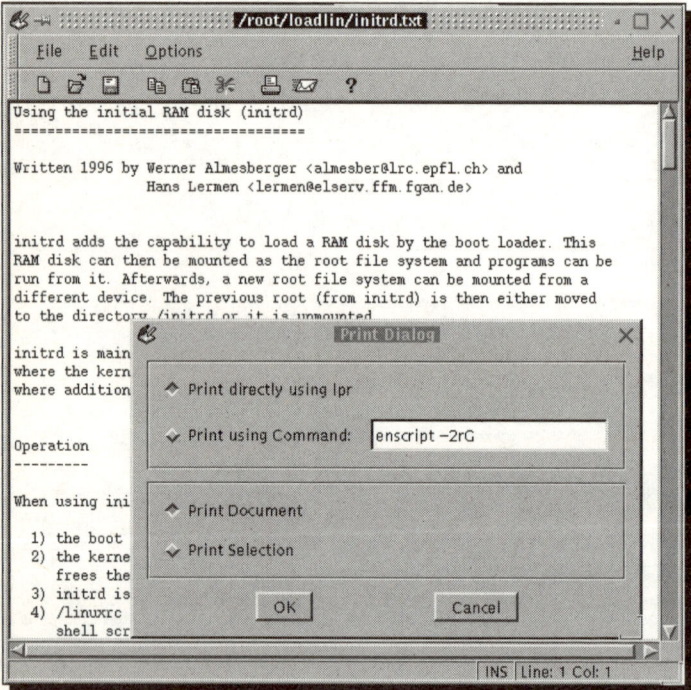

Fig. 7.9 Printing a KEdit Document

As you can see from the Print dialogue box, it is possible to select what you want to print; **Print Document** or **Print Selection**. For the latter choice you must first select the part of the document you want to print by highlighting it, before issuing the **Print** command.

Writing Simple Scripts

In the previous chapter (page 72), we discussed a technique of mounting an external hard disc drive as a DOS device, so that Windows/DOS files could be accessible to us from within Linux, and Linux files could be accessible to us from within Windows/DOS. If you remember, to achieve this we had to login as 'root', start up Shell every time we booted Linux and type in the relevant commands.

We will now show you a different way of doing the same thing; by writing the relevant commands in a script file, using the KEdit Text editor, then creating an icon on the desktop, which when clicked, will mount our external hard drive automatically. Of course, the method can be applied to other commands, so it is worth learning how to use it.

To begin the process, start KEdit and type the commands required to mount the external drive on one line, as shown below, and press the <Enter> key at the end of the line.

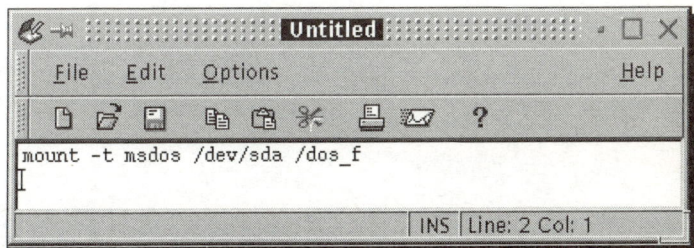

Fig. 7.10 Using KEdit to Write a Script

Having done so, use the **File, Save** command and save the 'untitled' script under the name **mount_dos_f**, as shown in Fig. 7.11, or you could give it another suitable name.

Next, use the kfm application, locate the newly saved file (in our case it is to be found in the root (/) directory), right-click it, and select the Properties option from the displayed shortcut menu. The Properties dialogue box has two tabs; **General** and **Permissions**.

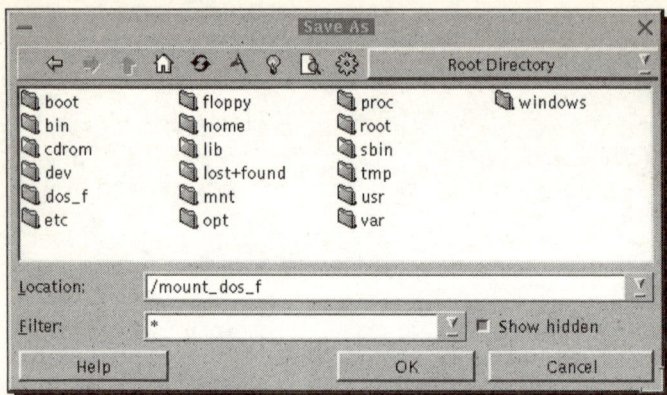

Fig. 7.11 Saving a Script File

Click the **Permissions** tab to display the following screen in which we have clicked the **User, Exec** box to make the file executable, and changes its icon from a 'page' to a 'cog' (you will see this next time you start the kfm application).

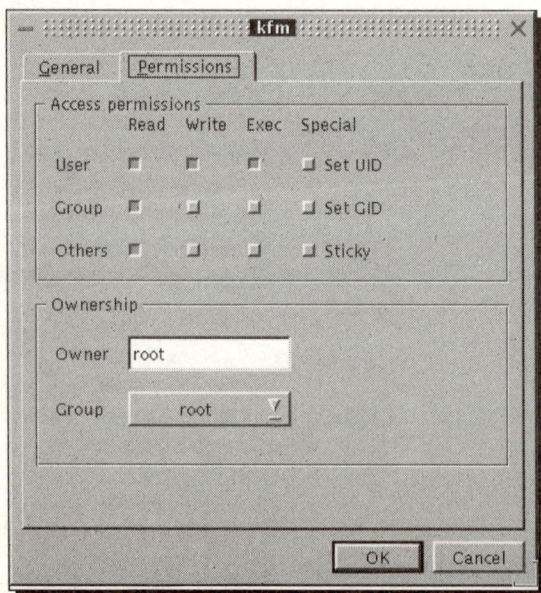

Fig. 7.12 Changing Access Permission of a Script File

Whenever we left-click this file in the future, it executes the code written in it and mounts our external hard drive as a DOS device. However, the way things stand, the procedure of starting kfm, locating the executable file and left-clicking it is rather too long-winded. Below, we show you a better method of doing all this in one move, by putting an icon on the desktop which whenever it is left-clicked, does the mounting automatically. This procedure, of course, can be applied to any other commands that we might want to execute.

So to start the process, left-click the Templates folder on the desktop, drag the icon of the **Program.kdelnk** file on the desktop, and select to copy it from the pop-up menu. Next, right-click the newly created Program icon and select **Properties** from the shortcut menu, to display the following.

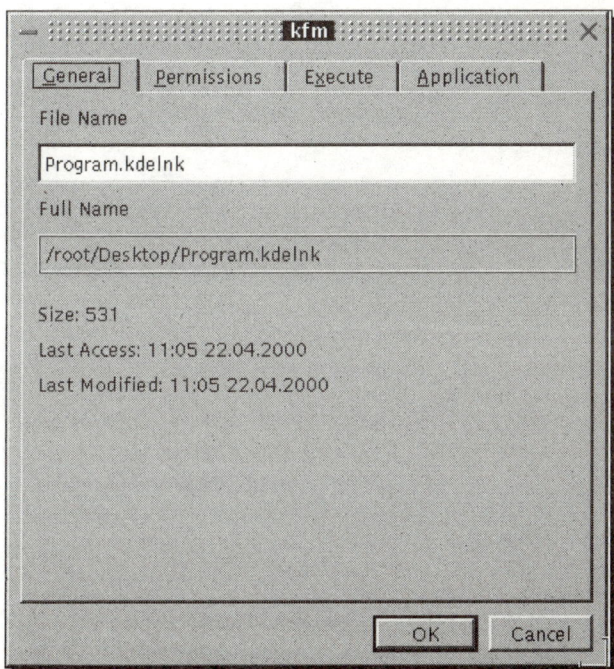

Fig. 7.13 Changing the Name of the Executable Link File

In the General tab box, change the name of the displayed file from **Program.kedlnk** to something more recognisable, say **Mount_DOS**. Next, click the Execute tab and **Browse** to the location and name of your executable file, which in our case was saved in the root (/) directory, as shown below.

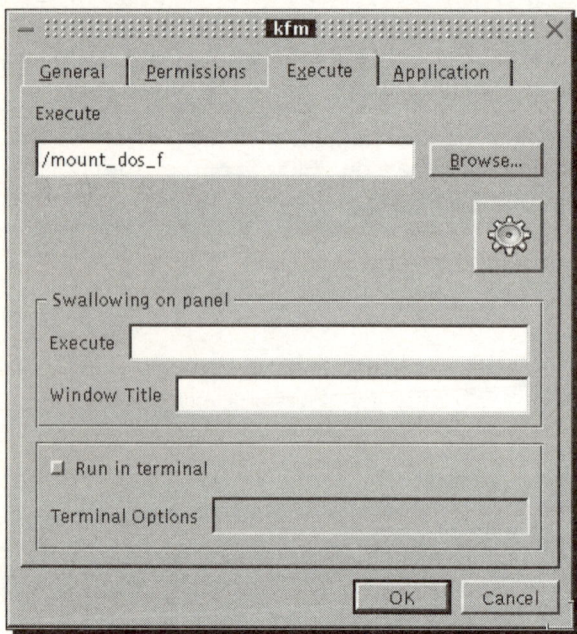

Fig. 7.14 Locating the Executable Script File

Note the file's icon, a 'cog', which indicates an executable file. Next, click on the cog icon to open up a window full of alternative icons, as shown on the next page. Select an appropriate icon to represent the application at hand (we chose the **zip_mount.xpm** icon which is to be found at the end of the list) and press the **OK** button, to take you back to the kfm screen in which you press the **OK** button once more.

Now you have a distinctive icon on your desktop and every time you start Linux you can click it to do the mounting for you automatically.

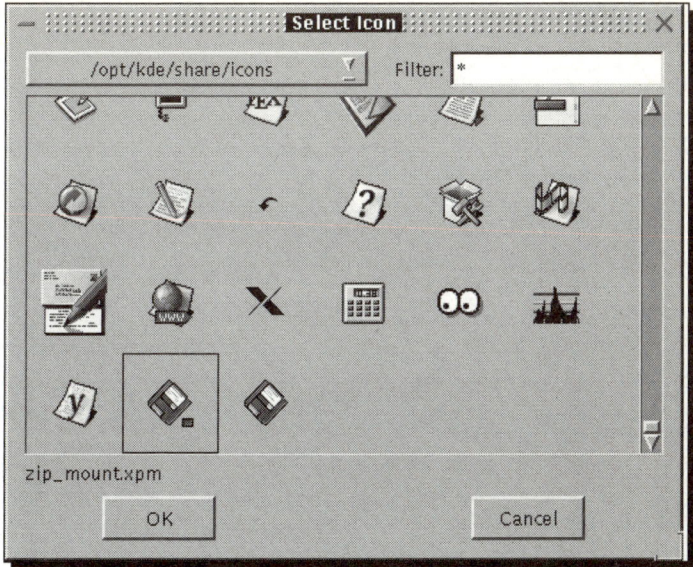

Fig. 7.15 Selecting an Alternative File Icon for a Script File

Our desktop now has two extra icons, as shown to the left in Fig. 7.16; one showing a mounted zip drive disc, the other a large red X - the red colour shows up better on the screen. The latter was created so that when it is left-clicked, it shuts down Linux automatically. Do try to write your own script file to do this, using the KEdit editor.

Do note that these additional two icons will only be on your desktop if you have logged in as 'root'.

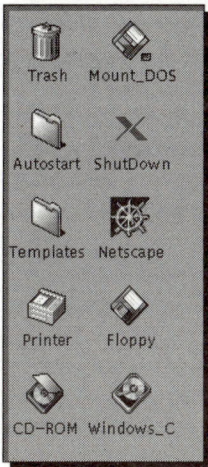

Fig. 7.16 Our Desktop with Executable Icons

The KWrite Editor

KWrite is a programmer's editor which can be used to read and write small text files, but is best used in conjunction with kfm for source file browsing for different programming languages. KWrite being a programmer's editor, can deal with the coloured syntax that some programming languages, such as C/C++, Java, HTML, etc., tend to adopt.

To start the editor, click the **K Start** button and select **Applications, Advanced Editor**. This opens the blank screen shown below.

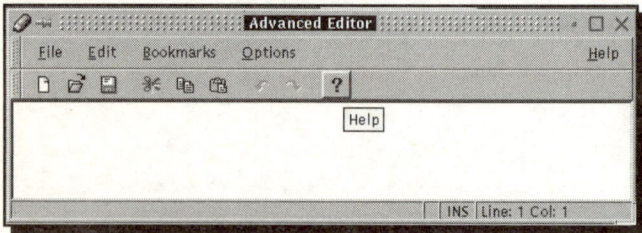

Fig. 7.17 KWrite's Opening Screen

To find out more about this advanced editor, click the large **?** (Help) icon on KWrite's Toolbar to display the KWrite Handbook. Do spend some time browsing through the various topics of this Handbook; it will tell you a lot about this advanced editor, including how to optimise it.

KWrite supports the 'drag and drop' protocol, which means that you can drag and drop files from the Desktop or kfm or some remote ftp site that you have opened in kfm, into KWrite. Furthermore, you can use KWrite to open and save files transparently on the Internet.

KWrite supports the Undo and Redo commands, as well as the Indent and Unindent commands, which can be extremely useful when writing programs in different computer languages. Files created within KWrite can be saved to disc in the normal way, but to print such files you will have to use kfm as KWrite does not support direct printing at present.

8

Other KDE Applications

The KOrganizer

The KOrganizer is an application that lets you organise and manage your time more effectively by allowing you to fill in and see at a glance an appointments and meetings diary. The program also allows you to produce 'To Do' lists. The Calendar can be viewed with a daily, weekly, or monthly format, and switching from one view to another, or to the 'To Do' list view, is simply done by clicking appropriate icons on the program's toolbar.

Starting the KOrganizer Program

To start the KOrganizer, click the **K Start** button then select the **Applications**, **Organizer** option on the cascade menu.

The KOrganizer can be used *online* or *offline*. To work online, your computer must be connected to a shared network resource, particularly if you are planning to use the Mail Appointments features. In that case, your computer must have a connection and a list of users on the system. You work offline if your computer hasn't a connection to a network, in which case the Mail Appointments features are not available to you.

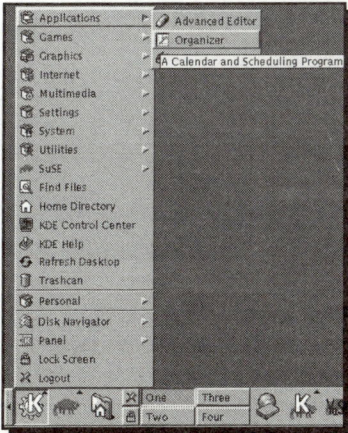

Fig. 8.1 Starting the KOrganizer

When you start the KOrganizer, the program first displays the screen shown in Fig. 8.2 below. The Calendar occupies the top left panel, with today's date marked in a blue square, while the bottom left panel displays the 'To Do' list for the day. On the right panel of the screen the Appointments list is displayed for the selected date, the default being today's date.

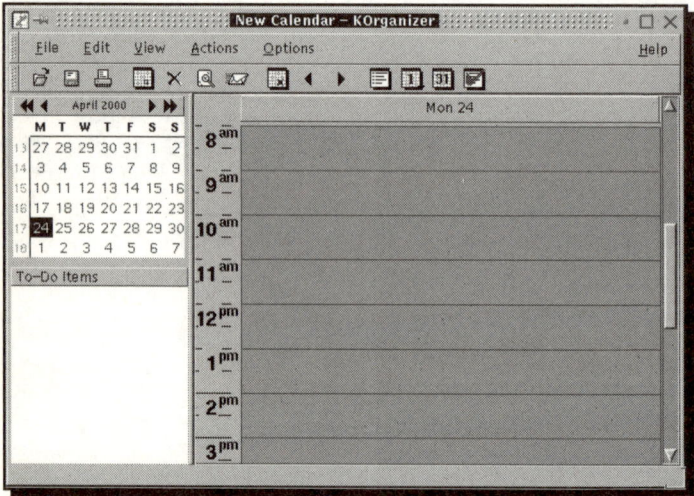

Fig. 8.2 The KOrganizer Opening Screen

As you can see, this program has some common screen elements with those of other Linux applications, even though at first glance it might look radically different. The central area of the KOrganizer window changes the way it displays according to which View is active.

To change the displayed view to another one, say from Calendar to To-do list, simply left-click the appropriate Toolbar icon as shown on the next page, or select the option from the **View** drop-down sub-menu.

The Toolbar icons on the KOrganizer screen have the following functions:

Toolbar Icon	*Function*
	Open a Calendar
	Save this Calendar
	Print
	New Appointment
	Delete Appointment
	Search for an Appointment
	Mail Appointment
	Go to Today
	Previous Day
	Next Day
	List View
	Schedule View
	Month View
	To-do List View

Clicking the Month icon on the Toolbar, displays the following view:

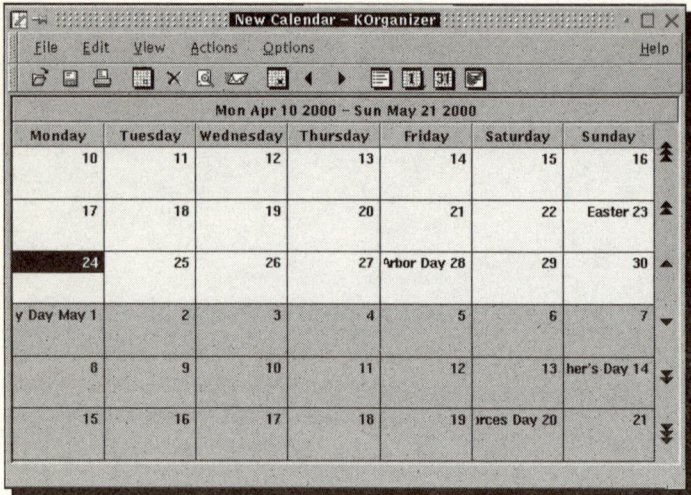

Fig. 8.3 KOrganizer's Month View

Obviously the font size here is far too large, because we cannot see the whole of the default holiday captions in this view. To change the font size, use the **Options, Edit Options** menu command and select **Fonts** on the left panel of the displayed Configuration dialogue box shown in Fig. 8.4. Next, click the **Month view font** button on the right panel and change the size of the font from 10 to 6, and press **OK**.

Other fonts of other entries could be changed from this dialogue box to meet your requirements. Also, you might want to change, for example, the Time & Date format, so that dates appear in Day.Month.Year format, and the Time Zone which is given as an offset from GMT. Finally, use the Configuration dialogue box to change your personal data, such as e-mail address, default country holidays, etc., and your printing preferences.

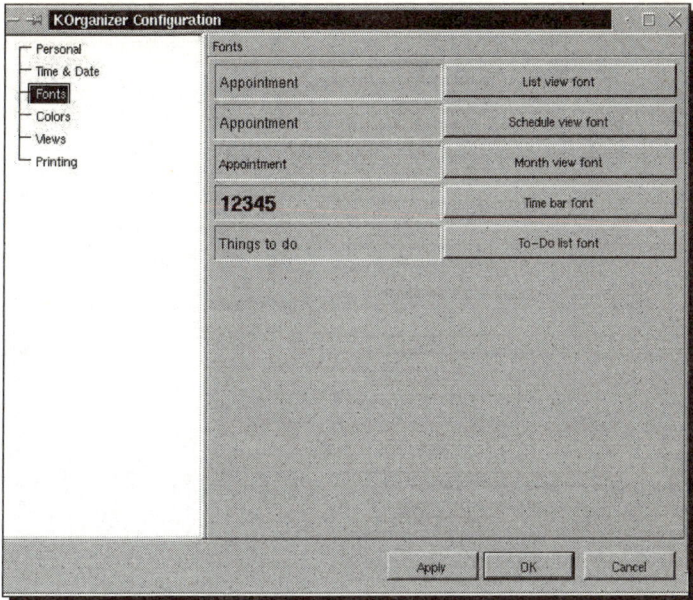

Fig. 8.4 KOrganizer's Configuration Dialogue Box

If any of the above changes are to take effect, remember to press the **Apply** button followed by **OK**. Both these buttons are at the bottom of the Configuration dialogue box, which may be out of your view as this window cannot be re-sized, so you may have to press the <Alt> key and move the dialogue box upwards with the left mouse button depressed.

To return to the weekly view, click the Schedule View icon on the Toolbar.

Entering Appointments

To see the facilities available within KOrganizer, let us enter an appointment for a meeting on Tuesday 25 April at 10.00 a.m. To do so, click on 25 April in either the Schedule view or the Monthly view, then either use the **Actions, New Appointment** command or click the New Appointment Toolbar icon to open the dialogue box shown in Fig. 8.5.

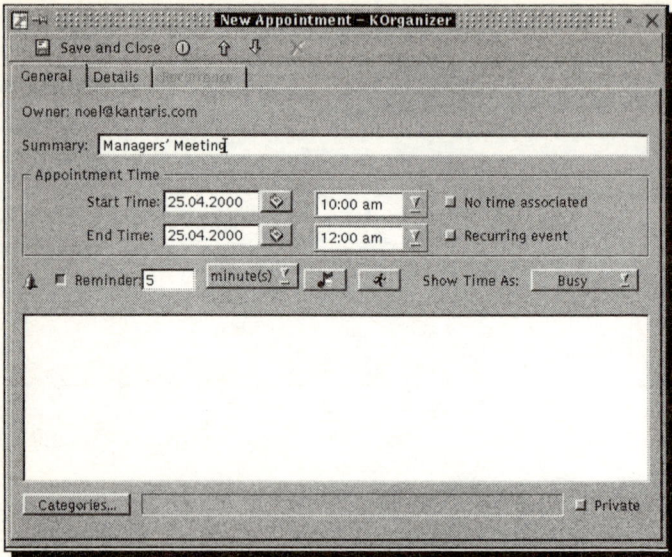

Fig. 8.5 KOrganizer's New Appointments Dialogue Box

You can now fill in the starting and finishing time of your appointment, and type in a few words to describe the type of meeting - say 'Managers' Meeting'. You can also select whether this appointment is a 'Recurring event', and/or whether a 'Reminder' is required.

At the bottom of the New Appointment dialogue box there is a **Categories** button which when pressed reveals a selection list from which you can choose the type of Category for your appointment. At the bottom right of the dialogue box you can specify whether this appointment is 'Private' or not.

Clicking the Details tab of the New Appointment dialogue box allows you to specify who should attend this meeting and type in information about the attendees. To return to the KOrganizer view you were in before you started to enter appointments, click the **Save and Close** icon at the top of the New Appointment dialogue box. If this is the first time you have used the KOrganizer, you will be asked for a filename to save your entries.

Note that after pressing the **Save and Close** icon, the entry is inserted in your diary, as shown below, and double-clicking within this entry area, displays the New Appointment dialogue box for the selection of further options.

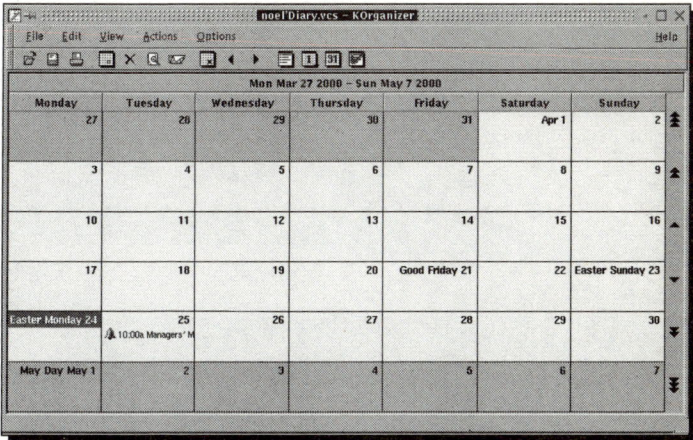

Fig. 8.6 KOrganizer's Month View Showing an Appointment

To edit or delete an entry, whether in the Schedule or Month view, right-click the entry and select an appropriate option from the displayed quick menu shown to the left. When you

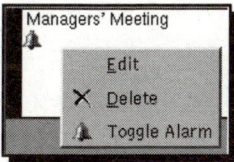

attempt to close KOrganizer, you will be reminded to save your entries, if you have not saved them already, with the opening of a Save As dialogue box.

We strongly advise you to look up the KOrganizer Reference Manual which can be reached from the **Help, Contents** menu command. It is a thorough manual with detailed explanations of all the menu commands, and information on how to configure KOrganizer to suit your needs.

To Do List

Tasks appear in the 'To Do' list, which you can either display in the Schedule view or the To-do List view. To create a task, right-click within the 'To-Do Items' area of the Schedule view and select the **New To-do** option from the displayed quick menu, as shown below in Fig. 8.7.

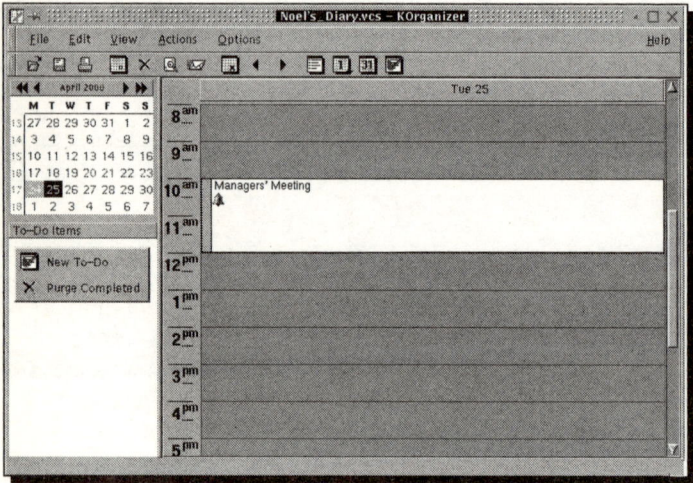

Fig. 8.7 Adding Items in Organizer's To-do List

This opens a numbered box in which you can type a short description of the task to be done.

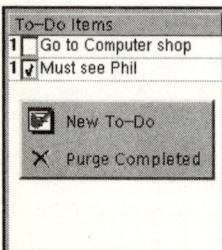

Fig. 8.8 Purging
Completed Tasks

Completed tasks can be marked by left-clicking the small square to the left of the task description. To delete completed tasks, simply right-click within the 'To-Do Items' area and select the **Purge Completed** option from the displayed quick menu, as shown to the left in Fig. 8.8.

The Address Book

The Address Book application allows you to keep a list of your contacts, their addresses, telephone numbers, fax numbers, and e-mail addresses, as shown below. To create entries in the address book, start the application, click the **K Start** button, then select **Utilities, Address book** from the cascade menu. This opens up the screen below.

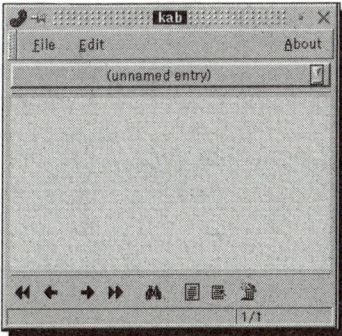

Fig. 8.9 Initial Address Book Window

The icons at the bottom of the kab (address book) window have the following function (from left to right):

◀◀ Go to first entry
◀ Go to previous entry
➡ Go to next entry
▶▶ Go to last entry
🔍 Search entries
▤ Add a new entry
▤ Change this entry
🗑 Remove this entry.

Pressing the ▤ 'Add a new entry' icon displays the New entry dialogue box shown below.

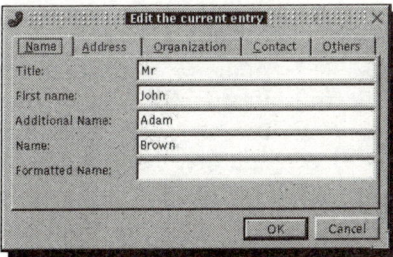

Fig. 8.10 Add or Edit an Entry

Fill in this dialogue box, starting with the Name tab window and working your way through all the other tab windows. The Name, Address, and Organization windows are self-explanatory, so go ahead and fill them in with the details of someone you know. On the next page, we explain the last two tab windows of the Address Book.

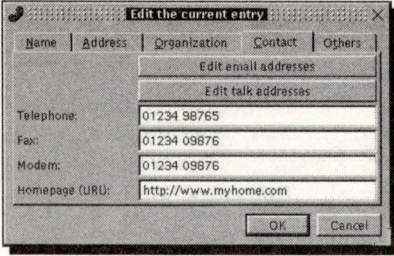

Fig. 8.11 Add information on contact

If you are connected to the Internet, you can get your computer to send an e-mail to any of your contacts, provided you have typed in their e-mail addresses in the Contact tab window shown in Fig. 8.11. You can do this in a pop-up window which is displayed when you click the 'Edit email addresses' bar. Finally, you can enter additional information on a given person (including their birthday) in the Others tab window. Pressing the **OK** button, displays the following information on the currently selected person.

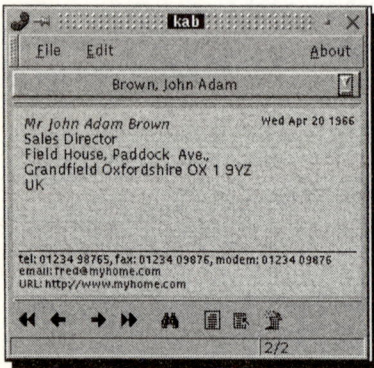

Fig. 8.12 Information on currently selected person

As you can see, everything you need to know about a person is shown here; name, address, date of birth (to the right of the name), telephone fax and modem numbers, e-mail and Web site address.

Entries in your Address Book can be found by using the search facility, then you can edit them or delete them. Finally, having selected an entry, pressing the **Edit** menu option, displays the sub-menu shown to the left. The last three options in this sub-menu allow you to **Mail** a message to the e-mail address of this person, **Talk** to the person, or **Browse** the person's Web site. Try it with real e-mail and Web site addresses.

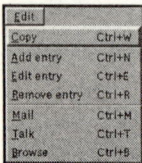

Having included a real e-mail address (use yours, not the one shown here), you can then test the system by using the **Edit, Mail** command which causes the KMail Composer application to be opened automatically, as shown below.

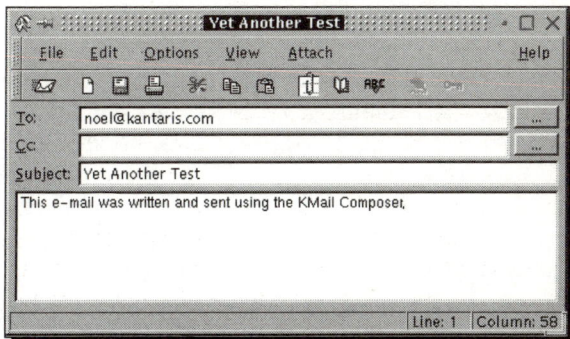

Fig. 8.13 The KMail Composer Window

The first time you use this facility the Settings dialogue box is displayed for you to fill in all the required information; similar to that used to configure Netscape (see page 62). Next, compose a short test message and send it to <u>your</u> e-mail address. A little while later, you can read your test e-mail using the KMail Composer **File, New Mailreader** menu command, to display the screen below.

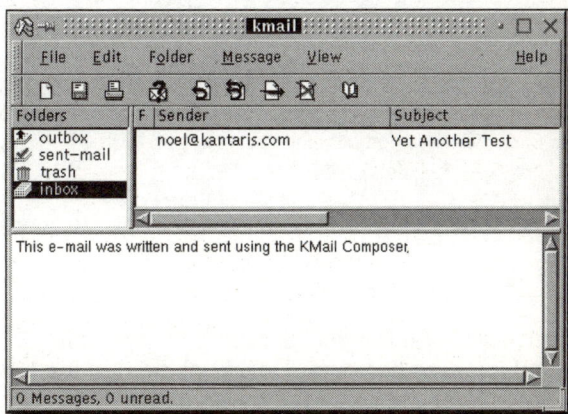

Fig. 8.14 The KMail Window

The Linux Paint Program

The current Paint program is a 32-bit Linux application, first introduced in 1997, but this is undergoing improvements as and when the author of the package finds time. You can use Paint to create, view and edit, simple graphics.

The current Paint version can now read and write an increased number of file formats, namely, (.bmp), (.jpeg), and (.gif) files, and also the xbm, xpm, and pnm formats.

Starting Paint

To start Paint, click the **K Start** button, then select **Graphics** from the cascade menu and click the **Paint** entry. The following 'untitled.gif' Paint opening window is then displayed.

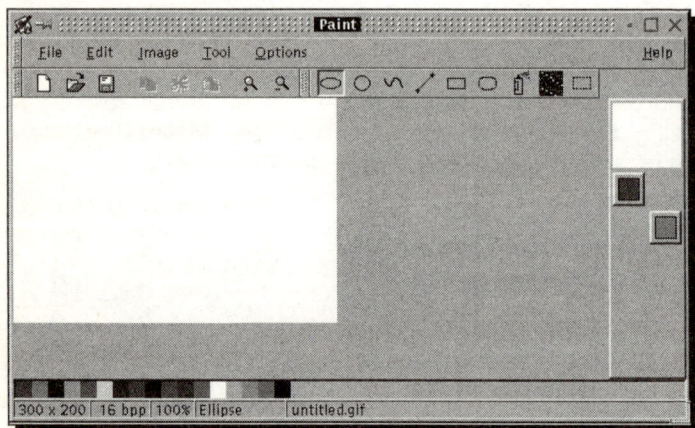

Fig. 8.15 The Opening Paint Window

The window is divided into a 'drawing' area, surrounded by the Menu bar, Toolbar, and Toolbox at the top, the Palette at the bottom, and the Display box and large foreground and background selection buttons at the right of the screen.

The Paint Toolbox

The drawing area is where you create your drawings with the help of various tools from the Toolbox. The function of both the Toolbar and Toolbox icons are flagged when you move the mouse pointer over them. Note that whichever tool was being used last session prior to closing Paint, is selected when you start Paint the next time.

To select a tool, simply point to it and left-click. Most tools work with either the current foreground or current background colours - using a tool to draw with the left mouse button depressed uses the foreground colour and with the right mouse button depressed uses the background colour.

More detail of the Toolbox functions is listed below in order of appearance from left to right.

Tool	*Function*
Ellipse	Used to draw hollow and filled ellipses, in the current foreground or background colour.
Circle	Used to draw hollow and filled circles, in the current foreground or background colour.
Pen	Used to draw freehand lines in either the foreground or background colour.
Line	Used to draw straight lines between two points in the current foreground or background colour.
Rectangle	Used to draw hollow and filled rectangles in the current foreground or background colour.
Rounded Rectangle	Used to draw hollow and filled rounded corner rectangles in the current foreground or background colour.

Spray Can	Used to produce a circular spray in the foreground or background colour.
Text	Used to add text in the current foreground colour, or background colour.
Area Selection	Used to select a rectangular area.

One can select to fill the different graphic shapes with a percentage of filled colour, which acts as a measure of transparency.

Preparing for a Drawing

Before you start drawing, you may need to set the size of the image you want. To do this, use the **Image**, **Resize** menu command to open the dialogue box below.

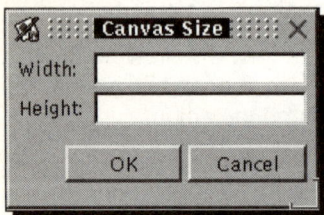

The default width and height settings of the previous canvas are given in pixels at the bottom of the Paint screen (see Fig. 8.15) as 300 x 200, together with the number of colours (16), and Paint Tool (Ellipse) being used at the time.

Fig. 8.16 The Canvas Size Box

The same dialogue box opens up if you use the **File, New Image** command, or click the New Canvas icon on the toolbar.

Selecting Working Colours

The current foreground and background colour settings are always shown in the two squares to the right of the screen, as shown on the next page.

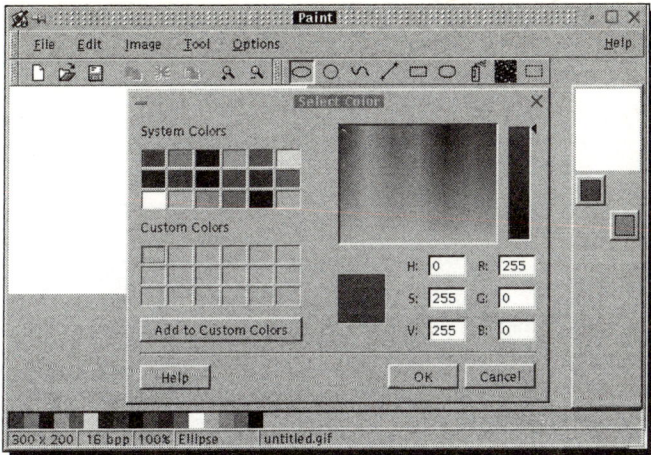

Fig. 8.17 Selecting Foreground and Background Colours in Paint

To select a new foreground or background colour, point to the appropriate large button to the right of the screen and click the left mouse button to open the Select Color dialogue box shown in Fig. 8.17. To select a different foreground or background colour to be used with any of the drawing tools in the Toolbox, left-click the colour in the System Colors palette of the dialogue box, or create a custom colour.

Using the Paint Tools

Most of the tools in the Paint Toolbox are quite easy and straightforward to use. To select a tool, point to it and click the left mouse button which depresses its icon in the Toolbox. To use them, move the pointer to a suitable position within the drawing area and drag the mouse pointer to accomplish the required task.

With most of the Toolbox options, dragging with the left mouse button uses the active foreground colour, and with the right button the active background colour. Releasing the mouse button stops the action being performed.

To change the tool's properties, use the **Tool, Tool Properties** menu command to open the two-tab dialogue box, shown in Fig. 8.18.

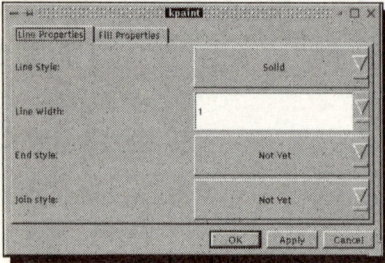

Fig. 8.18 The Draw Properties Box

From here, you can select the Line Properties and/or the Fill Properties of your drawings. With the Line Properties tab selected, you can choose the Line Style from Solid, Dashed, Dotted, etc., to None. You also select one of four line widths.

With the Fill Properties tab selected, you can choose to have such shapes as the ellipse, circle, rectangle, and rounded rectangle drawn hollow, filled, or with a certain percentage of fill. This latter choice gives the shapes being drawn a certain amount of transparency.

Entering Text in a Drawing

If you intend to enter text within a drawing, carry out the following steps:

- Select the Text tool from the Toolbox.

- Click the pointer on the working area to change the pointer to an insertion shape, then type the text.

* * *

Unfortunately, Paint is not a very accomplished application in its present form, therefore you are severely limited in what you can do with it. For example, you can not cut, copy, or paste either text or shapes, or move them around the drawing area. Furthermore, the selection tool doesn't appear to do anything at all! Perhaps by the time you read this, a new improved version of Paint might appear on the scene. We hope so!

Multimedia

Multimedia is one of the buzz words of this decade as far as personal computers are concerned. What is it? It's simply the ability to play sound, and images (both still and moving) through a computer, usually from a CD-ROM disc, a DVD disc, or downloaded from the Internet. In other words, almost a cross between a PC and a TV!

Linux has a multitude of 'hidden' features built into it to improve the PC's multimedia performance. These lead to a big improvement in both video and audio speed, quality and ease of use. As software developers bring out new programs to make use of these features we should see a transformation in this field.

Whether all the features described in the next few pages work on your PC will depend on your system. Most of them require at least a CD-ROM player, a graphics and sound card and speakers, to be fitted and correctly set up.

Games

We will not spend any time on this topic, but many people only seem to have a PC to use it for playing games! Our version of Linux placed 17 games in the Games folder. Most of these games come with quite good Help sections and we will leave it to you to explore them if you want.

The CD Player

The Kscd (which stands for the KDE simple CD player) application allows you to play music through your computer's CD-ROM drive. To start the application click the **K Start** button, then select **Multimedia, CD Player** from the cascade menu. This opens up the screen below.

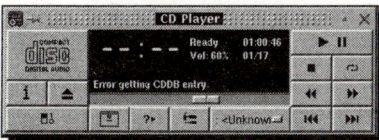

Those of you that like to listen to music while you work, should love the CD player.

Fig. 8.19 The CD Player

This is a must for an icon on the desktop; if you haven't mastered that technique yet, it is time you did! To see what all the buttons do, read the pop-up labels that appear when you move the mouse pointer over them.

If you cannot hear the music, make sure that the volume is turned up sufficiently high. This is controlled by the twin-button horizontal slider below the 'Error getting CDDB entry' message on the CD Player's screen (Fig. 8.19). To increase the volume, slide the button to the right; the volume is displayed in percentage on the screen - ours shows 60%.

If you still cannot hear the music, click the **K Start** button, then select **Multimedia, Sound Mixer Panel** from the cascade menu to display the following screen.

Fig. 8.20 The Sound Mixer Panel

Make sure that the volume slider (the leftmost vertical slider) is at its maximum position, as shown. Also, check that one of the two rightmost sliders, which represent the channel gain of your system is set correctly. Finally, adjust the horizontal slider at the bottom of the window which controls the relative volume between right and left speakers.

If you have any problems with your sound card (for example, it is not recognised automatically when you boot up Linux), then use the YaST2 System configuration program (see page 44), select the **Hardware/Sound** option from the displayed menu, and press the **Launch module** bar. After detection, you are even given the option to test your sound system there and then.

The message 'Error getting CDDB entry' appears on the CD Player screen because the system is set up by default to try to connect to a Compact Disc DataBase on the Internet.

To remove the error message, click on the Configure Kscd icon (the one with the hammer and screwdriver on it, to open the dialogue box below, and click on the 'Enable Remote CDDB' check box (top left of the screen) to disable the option.

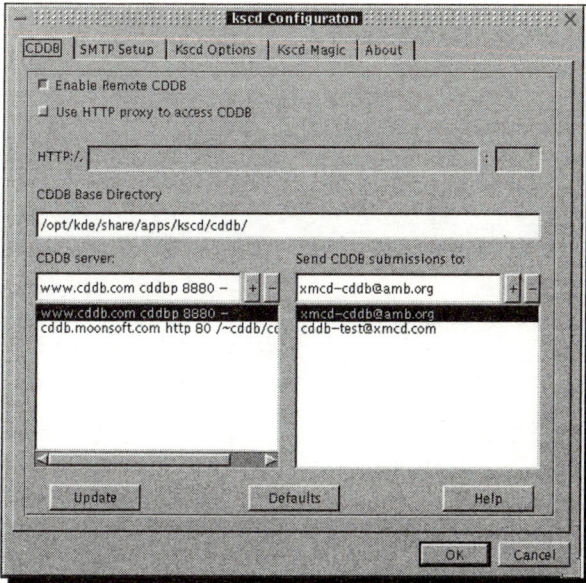

Fig. 8.21 The Kscd Configuration Screen

The Compact Disc DataBase, whether on an Internet site or on your hard disc, holds information on your specific CD; composer, title, and individual track titles. As each compact disc has a unique identification number, information relating to it can be found easily, while it is playing, and if it exists.

If this information is stored in one of the specified Internet sites, then you do not need to type it in yourself. If not, then there is only one way to proceed! Obviously, to download such details from the Internet, you need to be connected to it and you must configure your system accordingly using the dialogue box of Fig. 8.21. You are advised to have a close look at the help file displayed when the **Help** button on this dialogue box is clicked.

To enter information on a particular CD while it is playing, click the CDDB Dialog icon, the second icon to the left of the Configure Kscd icon, to display the CD Database Editor dialogue box shown below.

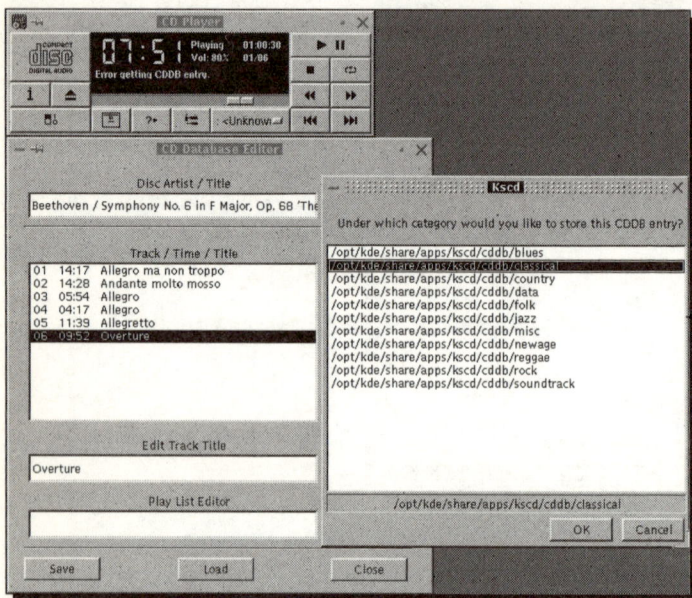

Fig. 8.22 The Kscd Configuration Screen

In Fig. 8.22 above, we show the process of typing in the required information, then saving it to disc. First, type in the composer and disc title in the 'Disc Artist / Title' box, separating composer from title by a forward slash (/). Next, highlight each track in turn in the 'Track / Time / Title' box, and type in the 'Edit Track Title' box the title of each highlighted track. Pressing the <Enter> key transfers this to the 'Track / Time / Title' box. When all tracks have been given titles, then click the **Save** button to save this information in an appropriately displayed folder - these are categorised according to type of music.

It is well worth spending some time entering the details of your favourite compact discs (or obtaining them from the Internet). Once such information has been entered (or downloaded) and saved, then the CD Player not only lists the track details as they play, but lets you jump to a particular named one, or to select a particular play order - not recommended with classical music!

If you managed to download information from the Internet relating to a particular CD and you feel obliged as a result, you could always clear your conscience by perhaps sending information that you laboriously compiled on a CD to a Web database to build up their system. After all, it is pointless repeating such a huge effort if there is another, simpler communal way. Have fun!

9

Commands Summary

The following is a summary of the most useful commands, from the user's point of view, supported by the Linux operating system. For a full list of command qualifiers, consult your system's documentation, or type the command

```
man command_name
```

in a *Shell*, where **man** stands for the reference 'manual'.

Command	Description / Explanation
at [qualifiers]	Executes a command or script at a specified time. **at** and **batch** read commands from standard input to be executed at a later time. **at** allows you to specify when the commands should be executed, while jobs queued with **batch** will execute as soon as possible.

Qualifiers:

−c	C shell. **csh** is used to execute *script*.
−s	Standard (Bourne) shell. **sh** is used to execute the job.
−m	Mail. Send mail after the job has been run.
−r *jobs*	Removes the specified *jobs* which were previously scheduled by **at** or **batch**.

	−q *queue*	Submit the job in queue (d-z) rather than the default queue a. **batch** submits jobs in queue b.
	script	is the name of a file to be used as command input.

atq [qualifiers]   Displays the queue of jobs to be run at specified times. With no qualifiers, the queue is sorted in chronological order of execution. If no usernames are specified, the entire queue is displayed; otherwise, only those jobs belonging to the named users are displayed.

Qualifiers:

−c   Creation time. Sorts the queue by the time that the **at** command was given, the most recent job first.

−n   Number of jobs. Prints the total number of jobs currently in the queue. Does not list them.

atrm [qualifiers]   Removes jobs spooled by **at** or **batch**

Qualifiers:

−f   Force. Suppresses all information regarding the removal of the specified jobs.

−i   Interactive. Asks if a job should be removed; a response of 'y' verifies this.

–	Removes jobs that were queued by the current user. If invoked by 'root' (super-user), the entire queue will be flushed.
job-number	Removes each *job-number* you specify.
username	Removes all jobs belonging to *username* provided that you own the indicated jobs. Jobs belonging to other users can only be removed by 'root' (super-user).

batch [qualifiers]   Executes a command or script at a specified time - see **at** command.

biff [qualifiers]   Gives notice of incoming mail messages. If notification is allowed, the terminal rings the bell and displays the header and the first few lines of each arriving mail message.

Qualifiers:

y   Allows mail notification for the terminal.

n   Disables notification for the terminal.

cat [qualifiers]   Concatenates (joins) a file or files and lists the result.

Qualifiers:

–n   No. of lines starting from 1.

–s   Eliminates consecutive blank lines.

Example: $ cat file1 file2

cd [directory]	Changes logged directory or folder.
	Example: $ cd /u/user1/docs
chgrp [qualifiers]	Changes the group ownership of a file. You must belong to the specified group and be the owner of the file, or be 'root' (super-user).

Qualifiers:

−f   Forces no error reporting.

chmod [mode]   Changes permissions to files and directories or folders.

Mode: [ugoa][+−=][rwxstugo]

where the optional characters within the various square brackets have the following meaning:

[ugoa]

u	user (owner).
g	group.
o	others.
a	all.

[+-=]

+	add permissions.
−	subtract permissions.
=	replace permissions.

[rwxstugo]

r	read.
w	write.
x	execute.
s	set owner or group identity.
t	save text.
ugo	user/group/others - permission to be taken from present mode.

Example: $ chmod go+r prog1.txt

Adds read permission to members of the group and others for the file Prog1.txt.

clear   Clears the terminal screen.

comm [qualifiers]   Compares two files for common lines.

Qualifiers:

−1 suppresses lines only in file1.
−2 suppresses lines only in file2.
−3 suppresses lines in both files.

Example: $ comm −12 file1 file2

Lists lines only common to both.

cp [qualifier]   Copies file1 (source) to file2 (destination).

Qualifier:

−i   Interactively protects destination file, if it already exists, from being overwritten.

Example: $ cp −i file1 file2

date   Displays date on the screen.

file   Determines the type of a file by examining its contents.

find [qualifiers]   Finds and lists a file or files.

Qualifiers:

−atime n   where n is number of days since last access.

−links n   with n number of links.

	−mtime n where n is No. of days since last modification.
	−name filename.
	−newer most recently modified.

Example: $ find −atime 3 −print

Lists all files (−print must be included) not accessed during the last 3 days.

finger	Displays information about users.
grep [qualifiers]	Searches a file for a pattern.

Qualifiers:

−c Prints the count of matches.

−n Lists line number with match.

Example: $ grep −n Hello filename

groups	Displays a user's group memberships
head	Prints first 10 lines in a file.
id	Prints the user name and ID, and group name and ID.
kill	Terminate background job.

Example $ kill job_number

last	Indicates last logins by user or terminal.
lpq [qualifiers]	Displays the queue of printer jobs.

Qualifiers:

−P *printer*   Displays information on the queue of the specified *printer*.

–l   Displays queue information in long format; includes the name of the host from which the job originated.

lpr [qualifiers]   Sends a job to the printer.

Qualifiers:

–P *printer*   Sends output to the named *printer*. Otherwise sends output to the printer named in the PRINTER environment variable, or to the default printer, lp.

lprm [qualifiers]   Removes jobs from the printer queue. Without any qualifiers, it deletes the job that is currently active, provided that the user who invoked **lprm** owns that job.

Qualifiers:

–P *printer*   Specifies the queue on a specified printer. Otherwise it uses the printer named in the PRINTER environment variable.

–   Removes all jobs owned by user. If invoked by a super-user, all jobs in the spool are removed.

ls [qualifiers]   Lists files in logged directory in alphabetical order.

Qualifiers:

–a all files.
–c in order of creation.

	−g give group identity.
	−l in long format.
	−s in block size.
	−t sorted by modification time.
	−u sorted on last access time.

Example: $ ls −acl

mail	Receives and sends mail.

Examples:

Receive: $ mail

Send: $ mail login_name(s)
               $ message
               $ Ctrl+d

man	Displays reference manual pages.

mesg [qualifiers]	Permits or denies the display of messages on the terminal screen.

Qualifiers:

n   denies display permission.
y   permits display.

mkdir	Makes (creates) a directory.

Example: $ mkdir docs

more	Lists contents of files a page at a time.

Example: $ more longfile

mv [qualifier]	Moves file1 (source) to file2 (destination) which renames a file.

Qualifier:

−i　Interactively protects destination file, if it already exists, from being overwritten.

Example: mv −i file1 file2

newgrp　Logs in to a new group. With no arguments, **newgrp** changes the group identification back to the group specified in the user's password file entry.

passwd　Changes password.

pr [qualifiers]　Prints a file.

Qualifiers:

−ln　where n is the page length (default is 66 lines).

−wn　where n is the page width (default 72 characters).

pwd　Prints working directory.

quota　Displays a user's disc quota and usage.

rm [qualifiers]　Removes files from directories.

Qualifiers:

−i　Interactively protects existing files.

−r　Recursively removes directory files.

Examples:　$ rm file1
　　　　　　　$ rm docs/file1

rmdir	Removes directory if empty.
rsh	Remote shell. Connects to the specified *hostname* and executes the specified *command*. If *command* is omitted, instead of executing a single command, **rsh** logs you in on the remote host using **rlogin**.

Example: $ rsh server mail

will inform you whether you have mail or not. The above line can be included in a batch file.

sort [qualifiers]	Sorts or merges files.

Qualifiers:

−b	Ignores blanks.
−d	Dictionary order.
−f	Fold upper to lower case.
−i	Ignores characters outside the printable ASCII set.
−n	Sorts numbers by value.
−o	Directs output to a file.
−r	Sorts in reverse order.

Example: $ sort −nr file.dta

tail n	Lists last n lines of a file, if n is negative, or starts listing on nth line, if n is positive.
talk	Talk is a visual communication program which copies lines from your terminal to that of another user.

time	Displays the execution time of a command.
users	Displays a compact list of logged-in users.
vim	Accesses the improved vi screen editor.
wc [qualifiers]	Counts number of lines, words and characters in a file.
	Qualifiers: −c Counts only characters. −l Counts only lines. −w Counts only words.
who	Who is logged in on the system.
write	Writes a message to another user.

10

Glossary of Terms

Account
A combination of *login* and *password*, normally created by the system administrator.

ActiveX
A set of technologies that enables software components to interact with one another in a networked environment, regardless of the language in which the components were created.

Add-in
A mini-program which runs in conjunction with another and enhances its functionality.

Address
A unique number or name that identifies a specific computer or user on a network.

Anonymous FTP
Anonymous FTP allows you to connect to a remote computer and transfer public files back to your local computer without the need to have a user ID and password.

Application
Software (program) designed to carry out certain activity, such as word processing, or data management.

Applet
A program that can be downloaded over a network and launched on the user's computer.

Archie	Archie is an Internet service that allows you to locate files that can be downloaded via FTP.
ASP	Active Server Page. File format used for dynamic Web pages that get their data from a server based database.
ASCII	A binary code representation of a character set. The name stands for 'American Standard Code for Information Interchange'.
Authoring	The process of creating web documents or software.
Backbone	The main transmission lines of the Internet, running at over 45Mbps.
Background process	If your Shell is occupied with only one process, this is called its *foreground* process. Most Shells also offer the ability to run processes in the background.
Backup	To make a back-up copy of a file or a disc for safekeeping.
Bandwidth	The range of transmission frequencies a network can use. The greater the bandwidth the more information that can be transferred over a network.
Banner	An advertising graphic shown on a Web page.
Bash	Linux's command line interface.
BBS	Bulletin Board System, a computer equipped with software and telecoms links that allow it to act as an information host for remote computer systems.

Beta test	A test of software that is still under development, by people actually using the software.
Bitmap	A technique for managing the image displayed on a computer screen.
Bookmark	A marker inserted at a specific point in a document to which the user may wish to return for later reference.
Booting	The sequence of computer operations from power-up to loading the kernel.
Browse	A button in some KDE dialogue boxes that lets you view a list of files and folders before you make a selection.
Browser	A program, like Netscape, that lets you view Web pages.
Buffer	A sort of an intermediate memory which enables you to speed up access to data being moved between different media and devices that operate at different speeds.
Bug	An error in coding or logic that causes a program to malfunction.
Button	A graphic element in a dialogue box or toolbar that performs a specified function.
Cache	An area of memory, or disc space, reserved for data, which speeds up downloading.
Card	A removable printed-circuit board that is plugged into a computer expansion slot.

CD-ROM

Compact Disc - Read Only Memory; an optical disc which information may be read from but not written to.

Chart

A graphical view of data that is used to visually display trends, patterns, and comparisons.

Click

To press and release a mouse button once without moving the mouse.

Client

A computer that has access to services over a computer network. The computer providing the services is a server.

Clipboard

A temporary storage area of memory, where text and graphics are stored with the KEdit cut and copy actions.

Command

An instruction given to a computer to carry out a particular action.

Command line

The process of working with Linux from a Shell.

Compile

The process of turning source code into an executable program.

Compressed file

One that is compacted to save server space and reduce transfer times. A typical Linux file extension for compressed files is .tar.

Configuration

A general purpose term referring to the way you have your computer set up.

Console

Used to be synonymous with *terminal*. In Linux you have a virtual console which allows you to use one screen for many independent running sessions.

Cookies	Files stored on your hard drive by your Web browser that hold information for it to use.
CPU	The Central Processing Unit; the main chip that executes all instructions entered into a computer.
Cursor	The character that marks the place for input on a computer screen.
Cyberspace	Originated by William Gibson in his novel 'Neuromancer', now used to describe the Internet and the other computer networks.
Database	A collection of data related to a particular topic or purpose.
Deamon	A process that runs in the background and performs a specified operation at predefined times or in response to certain events. Typical deamon processes include print queues and e-mail handlers.
Device	A device is accessed in Linux via special entries in the file system, which are located in the directory /dev/. These entries contain the device numbers with which the kernel can reach the device drivers.
Dial-up Connection	A popular form of Net connection for the home user, over standard telephone lines.
Direct Connection	A permanent connection between your computer system and the Internet.
Directories	Part of the filing system structure. Files and other directories are listed in a directory, also called a folder.

Distribution

A particular make of Linux, such as SuSE, or Red Hat.

Default

The command, device or option automatically chosen.

Desktop

The Linux working screen background, on which you place program icons, etc.

Device driver

A special file that must be loaded into memory for Linux to be able to address a specific procedure or hardware device.

Device name

A logical name used by Linux to identify a device, such as lp0 or ttyS0 for the parallel or serial ports.

Dialogue box

A window displayed on the screen to allow the user to enter information.

DNS

Short for Domain Name System which provides mappings between domain names and IP addresses.

Directory

An area on disc where information relating to a group of files is kept.

Disc

A device on which you can store programs and data.

Disconnect

To detach a drive, port or computer from a shared device, or to break an Internet connection.

Document

A file produced by an application program. When used in reference to the Web, a document is any file containing text, media or hyperlinks.

Domain

A group of devices, servers and computers on a network.

Domain Name

A Web site name, such as suse.com, that allows you to reference that

Internet site without knowing its true numerical address.

DOS	Disc Operating System. A collection of small specialised programs that allow interaction between user and computer.
Double-click	To quickly press and release a mouse button twice.
Download	To transfer to your computer a file, or data, from another computer.
DPI	Dots Per Inch - a resolution standard for laser printers.
Drag	To move an object on the screen by pressing and holding down the left mouse button while moving the mouse.
Editor	A program for writing and changing text. Well known editors on Linux are GNU *emacs* and *vim*.
Engine	Software used by search services.
E-mail	Electronic Mail - A system that allows computer users to send and receive messages electronically.
Ethernet	A very common method of networking computers in a LAN.
FAQ	Frequently Asked Questions - A common feature on the Internet, FAQs are files of answers to commonly asked questions.
File	In Linux a file is the central concept for handling data. Files are used to write data onto mass-storage media, such as a hard disc.

File extension	The suffix following the period in a filename. For example .bmp indicates a graphics bitmap file.
Filename	The name given to a file.
Filesystem	A system for structuring files.
Filter	A set of criteria that is applied to data to show a subset of the data.
Firewall	Security measures designed to protect a networked system from unauthorised access.
Floppy disc	A removable disc on which information can be stored magnetically.
Folder	An area used to store a group of files, usually with a common link.
Font	A graphic design representing a set of characters, numbers and symbols.
Freeware	Software that is available for downloading and unlimited use without charge.
FTP	File Transfer Protocol. The procedure for connecting to a remote computer and transferring files.
Function key	One of the series of 10 or 12 keys marked with the letter F and a numeral, used for specific operations.
Gateway	A computer system that allows otherwise incompatible networks to communicate with each other.
GIF	Graphics Interchange Format, a common standard for images on the Web.

GNU	A complete free software system that is upwardly compatible with UNIX. GNU stand for 'GNU's Not UNIX'.
Graphic	A picture or illustration, also called an image. Formats include GIF, JPEG, and BMP.
Graphics card	A device that controls the display on the monitor and other allied functions.
GUI	A Graphic User Interface, such as Linux's KDE, the software front-end meant to provide an attractive and easy to use interface.
GZIP	A method of compressing and uncompressing Linux files.
Hard copy	Output on paper.
Hard disc	A device built into the computer for holding programs and data.
Hardware	The equipment that makes up a computer system, excluding the programs or software.
Help	A Linux system that gives you instructions and additional information on using a program.
Hit	A single request from a web browser for a single item from a web server.
Home directory	The starting point for most user activities on the machine. This is the directory or folder where a user keeps his/her private files.
Home page	The document displayed when you first open your Web browser, or the first document you come to at a Web site.

Host	Computer connected directly to the Internet that provides services to other local and/or remote computers.
Host	A computer acting as an information or communications server.
HTML	HyperText Markup Language, the format used in documents on the Web.
Hyperlink	A segment of text, or an image, that refers to another document on the Web, an Intranet or your PC.
Hypertext	A system that allows documents to be cross-linked so that the reader can explore related links, or documents, by clicking on a highlighted symbol.
Icon	A small graphic image that represents a function or object. Clicking on an icon produces an action.
Image	See graphic.
Insertion point	A flashing bar that shows where typed text will be entered into a document.
Interface	A device that allows you to connect a computer to its peripherals.
Internet	The global system of computer networks.
Intranet	A private network inside an organisation using the same kind of software as the Internet.
IP	Internet Protocol - The rules that provide basic Internet functions.
IP Address	Internet Protocol Address - Every computer on the Internet has a unique identifying number.

IP Routing	Internet Protocol Routing - The process of receiving an IP packet addressed to somewhere else and sending it on its way.
ISDN	Integrated Services Digital Network, a telecom standard using digital transmission technology to support voice, video and data communications applications over regular telephone lines.
ISP	Internet Service Provider - A company that offers access to the Internet.
JPEG/JPG	Joint Photographic Experts Group, a popular cross-platform format for image files.
KDE	A powerful graphical desktop environment that looks a little like Windows.
Kernel	The basic functions of any operating system, including memory management, multitasking, and input/output operations
Kilobyte	(KB); 1024 bytes of information or storage space.
LAN	Local Area Network - High-speed, privately-owned network covering a limited geographical area, such as an office or a building.
Laptop	A portable computer small enough to sit on your lap.
LCD	Liquid Crystal Display.
LILO	LInux LOader - A program used to boot Linux.

Links	The hypertext connections between Web pages.
Local	A resource that is located on your computer, not linked to it over a network.
Location	An Internet address.
Log on	To gain access to a network.
Makefile	A file that contains the commands required to compile source code into its final executable form.
Man page	Manual page - Refers to the Help files that come with your Linux distribution.
MBR	Master Boot Record - The first physical sector (cylinder 0, head 0, sector 1) of the first hard drive in the system.
Megabyte	(MB); 1024 kilobytes of information or storage space.
Megahertz	(MHz); Speed of processor in millions of cycles per second.
Memory	Part of computer consisting of storage elements organised into addressable locations that can hold data and instructions.
Menu	A list of available options in an application.
Menu bar	The horizontal bar that lists the names of menus.
MIDI	Musical Instrument Digital Interface - enables devices to transmit and receive sound and music messages.
MIME	Multipurpose Internet Mail Extensions, a messaging standard that allows Internet users to exchange

e-mail messages enhanced with graphics, video and voice.

MIPS

Million Instructions Per Second; measures speed of a system.

Mode

Refers to the attributes of a file, whether Read, Write, or Executable.

Modem

Short for Modulator-demodulator device. A device that lets computers communicate electronically.

Module

Software that can be loaded and unloaded as needed while your operating system is running.

Monitor

The display device connected to your PC, also called a screen.

Mounting

Describes the mounting of file systems into the directory tree of the system.

Mouse

A device used to manipulate a pointer around your display and activate processes by pressing buttons.

MS-DOS

Microsoft's implementation of the Disc Operating System for PCs.

Multimedia

The use of photographs, music and sound and movie images in a presentation.

Multitasking

Performing more than one operation at the same time.

Multi-user

An operating system that allows more than one person to work on the same machine.

Network

Two or more computers connected together to share resources.

Network server	Central computer which stores files for several linked computers.
NFS	A protocol required to access file systems on networked machines.
Node	Any single computer connected to a network.
Online	Having access to the Internet.
On-line Service	Services such as America On-line and CompuServe that provide content to subscribers and usually connections to the Internet.
Open source	The movement which advocates that software should be non-proprietary
Operating system	Software that runs a computer.
Page	An HTML document, or Web site.
PAP	Password Authentication Protocol supported by PPP
Password	A unique character string used to gain access to a network, program, or mailbox.
PATH	The location of a file in the directory tree.
Peripheral	Any device attached to a PC.
Perl	A popular language for programming CGI applications.
Pixel	A picture element on screen; the smallest element that can be independently assigned colour and intensity.
Plug-and-play	Hardware which can be plugged into a PC and be used immediately without configuration.

POP	Post Office Protocol - a method of storing and returning e-mail.
Port	The place where information goes into or out of a computer, e.g. a modem might be connected to the serial port.
PPP	Point-to-Point Protocol - One of two methods (see SLIP) for using special software to establish a temporary direct connection to the Internet over regular phone lines.
PPPD	Point-to-Point Protocol Deamon. A program that deals with connecting the PPP directly.
Print queue	A list of print jobs waiting to be sent to a printer.
Program	A set of instructions which cause a computer to perform tasks.
Prompt	The place where the user can type commands to the operating system.
Protocol	A set of rules or standards that define how computers communicate with each other.
Queue	A list of e-mail messages waiting to be sent over the Internet, or of files waiting to be sent to the printer.
RAM	Random Access Memory. The computer's volatile memory. Data held in it is lost when power is switched off.
Resource	A directory, or printer, that can be shared over a network.
Robot	A Web agent that visits sites, by requesting documents from them, for the purposes of indexing for search

	engines. Also known as Wanderers, Crawlers, or Spiders.
ROM	Read Only Memory. A PC's non-volatile memory. Data is written into this memory at manufacture and is not affected by power loss.
Root	The person responsible for maintaining and supervising a complex system or network.
Root directory	The top level directory, or folder, of a file system.
Runlevel	A runlevel describes a certain operating state of the system.
Script	Allows you to automate complex sequences of instructions. Similar to a DOS batch file.
Scroll bar	A bar that appears at the right side or bottom edge of a window.
Search	Submit a query to a search engine.
Search engine	A program that helps users find information across the Internet.
Serial interface	An interface that transfers data as individual bits.
Server	A computer system that manages and delivers information for client computers.
Shared resource	Any device, program or file that is available to network users.
Shareware	Software that is available on public networks and bulletin boards. Users are expected to pay a nominal amount to the software developer.
Shell	Another term for user interface.

Signature file	An ASCII text file, maintained within e-mail programs, that contains text for your signature.
Site	A place on the Internet. Every Web page has a location where it resides which is called its site.
SLIP	Serial Line Internet Protocol, a method of Internet connection that enables computers to use phone lines and a modem to connect to the Internet without having to connect to a host.
SMTP	Simple Mail Transfer Protocol - a protocol dictating how e-mail messages are exchanged over the Internet.
Socket	An endpoint for sending and receiving data between computers.
Software	The programs and instructions that control your PC.
Source code	The high-level instructions by which a program is written.
Spamming	Sending the same message to a large number of mailing lists or newsgroups. Also to overload a Web page with excessive keywords in an attempt to get a better search ranking.
Spider	See robot.
Spooler	Software which handles transfer of information to a store to be used by a peripheral device.
SSH	Secure Shell - A program developed by SSH Communications Security that lets you log into a remote

	computer over a network to execute commands and to move files from one machine to another.
SSL	Secure Sockets Layer, the standard transmission security protocol developed by Netscape, which has been put into the public domain.
Standard input/output	Every process inherits three channels where it can read and write data. These are standard input (stdin), standard output (stdout), and standard error (stderr). Normally, Stdin is set to the keyboard, while stdout and stderr to the screen, although they can be redirected by means of the Shell.
Subscribe	To become a member of.
Surfing	The process of looking around the Internet.
SVGA	Super Video Graphics Array; it has all the VGA modes but with 256, or more, colours.
Swap file	An area of your hard disc used to store temporary operating files, also known as virtual memory.
Switch	Used to change the default behaviour of programs. For example, in the command line you can type a command name followed by an optional switch.
Sysop	System Operator - A person responsible for the physical operations of a computer system or network resource.
System administrator	See Root.

TAR	A method of compressing files.
TCP/IP	Transmission Control Protocol/Internet Protocol, combined protocols that perform the transfer of data between two computers. TCP monitors and ensures the correct transfer of data. IP receives the data, breaks it up into packets, and sends it to a network within the Internet.
Telnet	A program which allows people to remotely use computers across networks.
Terminal	A combination of a screen and keyboard without computing capabilities.
Text file	An unformatted file of text characters saved in ASCII format.
Thread	An ongoing message-based conversation on a single subject.
Tool	Software program used to support Web site creation and management.
Toolbar	A bar containing icons giving quick access to commands.
Toggle	To turn an action on and off with the same switch.
UNC	Universal Naming Convention - A convention for files that provides a machine independent means of locating the file that is particularly useful in Web based applications.
UNIX	Multitasking, multi-user computer operating system, developed by AT&T Labs in 1969, that is run by many computers that are connected to LANs of the Internet.

Upload/Download	The process of transferring files between computers. Files are uploaded from your computer to another and downloaded from another computer to your own.
URL	Uniform Resource Locator, the addressing system used on the Web, containing information about the method of access, the server to be accessed and the path of the file to be accessed.
Usenet	Informal network of computers that allow the posting and reading of messages in newsgroups that focus on specific topics.
User ID	The unique identifier, usually used in conjunction with a password, which identifies you on a computer.
Virtual Reality	Simulations of real or imaginary worlds, rendered on a flat two-dimensional screen but appearing three-dimensional.
Virus	A malicious program, downloaded from a web site or disc, designed to wipe out information on your computer.
W3C	The World Wide Web Consortium that is steering standards development for the Web.
WAIS	Wide Area Information Server, a Net-wide system for looking up specific information in Internet databases.
WAN	Wide Area Network - Connects computers that are separated over a wide area.

Web	A network of hypertext-based multimedia information servers. Browsers are used to view any information on the Web.
Web Page	A document that is accessible on the Web.
Webmaster	One whose job it is to manage a web site.
Wildcards	The character '*' and '?' that are used to stand for many characters or one character, respectively in commands, filenames, or search strings.
Window	Windows are usually rectangular screen segments which are decorated by a frame.
Windows	Microsoft's Graphical User Interface to their PC operating system.
Window manager	The program that is responsible (among other things) for the way a window looks and provides you with the ability to re-size, move and close it.
X Windows	A graphical user interface for UNIX and UNIX-like systems.

Index

Notes

Companion Discs

COMPANION DISCS are available for most computer books written by the same author(s) and published by BERNARD BABANI (publishing) LTD, as listed at the front of this book (except for those marked with an asterisk). These books contain many pages of file/program listings.

There is no Companion Disc for this book.

To obtain companion discs for other books, fill in the order form below, or a copy of it, enclose a cheque (payable to **P.R.M. Oliver**) or a postal order, and send it to the address given below. **Make sure you fill in your name and address** and specify the book number and title in your order.

Book No.	Book Name	Unit Price	Total Price
BP		£3.50	
BP		£3.50	
BP		£3.50	
Name .... Address		Sub-total	£.............
		P & P (@ 45p/disc)	£.............
		Total Due	£.............
Send to: P.R.M. Oliver, CSM, Pool, Redruth, Cornwall, TR15 3SE			

PLEASE NOTE